Growing in God's Direction

153 Inspired Words

Ruth Tschudin

ISBN 9780981927619
Library of Congress Control Number: 2012902195

Cover Design and Layout: Andrea Gelmini www.gelminidesign.com

Table of Contents

Heal

Yesterday I took my dog, Jessie, for a nice winter walk... and ended up slipping on black ice in front of our house, hitting the asphalt really hard, and breaking my wrist. So my husband, Hugo, and I found ourselves spending New Year's Eve in the emergency room. At our stage of life (he's 80 years old and I'm 66) our New Year's Eve is generally a stay-at-home-as-usual evening but this year it turned out to be an extremely unusual evening. During my entire life I never had so much as a fracture or a broken bone, but last night that record was shattered--along with my wrist.

Throughout my ordeal--lying on our sofa with an ice pack on the lump that now forced my left hand into an awkward position, fighting nausea and blackout, traveling to the emergency room for a series of extremely uncomfortable x-rays, getting a temporary bandage and splint administered--one God-given word, heal, came to my rescue. On and off I talked to my throbbing arm, silently and steadily bathing it, from elbow to finger tips, in a soothing, one-word treatment that went like this: heal, heal, heal, heal... Each time I did this I noticed an improvement.

Chances are I'll need surgery in a few days, but meanwhile I have a wonderful start on my draw-closer-to-God project. I wouldn't have chosen this experience, but with it comes an awareness of how much I have to be thankful for: a partner who willingly and cheerfully becomes my left hand, a hospital with skilled doctors and nurses who truly care, and a God who not only created us and gave us life, but also provides us with inner strength and a word of healing as needed.

O Great Physician, Heavenly Father, how awesome it is
  to feel Your presence and acknowledge your healing love;
    to know that you are there for us, no matter what.

Jesus, great teacher, healer, savior...
  You, too, are with us, as we read about you, pray to you
    and commit our lives to following you.

Holy Spirit, God within us, comforter and friend...
  Enlighten us, guide us, fill us with your healing touch
    so we can bless others with health-producing words and actions.

What About You?

1. When have surprises (good or bad) taken you down new roads, presenting unanticipated problems—and blessings?

2. How have God and others been there for you (and you for others) when challenges and changes mean pain, resentment, anxiety, etc.?

3. What pleasant words come to *your* mind--right now, as you read this?

Envision

January 3, 2010

What a great word for any day of the year! It's a harbinger of dreams-come-true because what we envision exerts a tremendous pull on our lives. I know, because two of the four things I envisioned and put into my computer's see-through mouse pad years ago have actualized. One was of our daughter, Elisa, finding her ideal life's partner. And now we not only have that, but our ideal grandbaby, too! We have also progressed toward the Kids'n'Kritters vision for our charitable organization, Open Doors, an Amazing Grace Foundation (a non-profit entity we started in 1999 to honor my mom and glorify God by helping those in need.)

We started helping animals as well as people in 2007 because of what I'm sure was a God-given vision. I clearly saw a dog named Jessie pulling children in a wagon. This related to my "Dare to Dream" idea of a development of cozy homes for children and animals in need of loving families. I took my first step by volunteering at a Children's Aid pre-adoptive treatment home. Then I found and adopted my Jessie, a senior dog abandoned by her lifelong family. Together we wrote a book called: "Bark Up the Right Tree, Lessons from a Rescued Dog." Through Amazon.com, the local bookstore, and Open Doors events we've sold hundreds of copies—to promote animal rescue and offer people practical life lessons.

TV preacher Joel Osteen says that "sight" is what we can see and "vision" is what can be. If God plants a dream in our hearts, we should go for it! So, this year Hugo and I are aiming for the third vision on my mouse pad: a place in Florida. He prefers Sanibel, a costly location on the Gulf of Mexico, ideal for his early-morning jogs on the beach. I lean toward the east coast, which is much more affordable and close to our daughter Elisa and family.

With you, all things are possible, Lord.
Enlarge our visions, expand our souls
so we can see and follow the path you have set for us.

Open our eyes, open our ears, open our hearts.
Forgive us, strengthen us, and
lead us in the way everlasting.

I see it, Lord… dreams you have for me:
drawing closer to you each day, and bringing others closer, too.
And doing it all for your glory. Let it be, dear Lord, let it be.

What About You?

1. What has happened in your life because you first envisioned it? What are some great dreams-come-true that others have achieved?

2. The fourth vision on my mouse pad is a retreat house in Ocean Grove, NJ, for Open Doors to use for God's good purposes. What visions or dreams, not yet realized, are calling *your* name?

3. My mouse pad has four sayings spread among the visions. They are: *Feel the joy! Praise the Lord! See the good!* and *Live/Laugh/Love!* What can we do right now to make this present moment, a precious gift from a loving Father, more enjoyable and fulfilling?

Relax

January 4, 2010

The operative word for today is relax—or perhaps we should call it "non-operative" because it entails letting go of both physical and mental activities in favor of the peace that passes understanding (Philippians 4:7). Thanks to today's word, I was an ideal candidate for a manual manipulation of my broken wrist rather than needing the operation predicted by the emergency room orthopedist. It was agony having that arm stretched, weighted down as it hung by two fingers, numbed by shots of Novocain, then twisted to reset the broken wrist, but I'm grateful that we went that route and avoided the operation. Thoughts of Jesus hanging on the cross helped me to get through a horrible five or ten minutes (which paled in light of the pain he bore for us).

A book I'm now reading during my morning quiet time is called "God Isn't in a Hurry, Learning to Slow Down and Live," by Warren Weirsbe—something sorely needed by a type-A personality like me. So, when the doctor told me to "relax" this morning I chuckled inwardly—because, little did he know, I'd already been nicely marinated in that direction. His advice only confirmed that this special word would indeed save the day for me. And it did.

When we got back home with my wrist securely "set," the sun was shining and I was tempted to take our dog, Jessie, for another frigid-weather walk to satisfy my hurt ego: "I'll show that hideous black ice it can't get the best of me!" But the Novocain was wearing off and I realized I'd do better to heed today's word. And because I'd gotten my marching (non-marching?) orders from above I didn't feel at all bad about asking Kim, our vacation dog-walker, to come over and exercise Jessie while I rested. Ahhh!

Things change for the better when we cast our cares on you, Lord,
when we rest in your everlasting arms,
when we put our full trust in you.

"Let go and let God," said positive thinker Norman Vincent Peale.
I also recall him quoting this verse from Isaiah (23:3a):
"Thou wilt keep him in perfect peace whose mind is stayed on thee."

Just as you blessed Dr. & Mrs, Peale during their faithful ministry,
so bless all of us who seek the equanimity and peace
that only you can provide.

What About You?

1. We painted Jesus' words, *Come unto me, all ye that labor and are heavy laden, and I will give you rest (Matthew 11:28)* above our bedroom door. What other Scriptures or sage advice can help us to maintain a healthful equanimity?

2. God restoreth my soul with beautiful views, songs in our Jacuzzi tub, and warmth from our gas fireplace. What helps you to relax and feel God's presence?

3. What are some ways of letting go and letting God?

Thank

January 5, 2010

As I lay in bed upon awakening this morning, waves of thankfulness swept through me. I thought of loved ones, our home, our country, Jesus' saving love...and of course my healing wrist. In Romans 8:28 Paul tells us that all things work together for good to those who love the Lord and are following his call. I can't say I've been a model follower, but I have certainly found many, many blessings in both the ups and downs of my life.

So once again I felt the word of the day (*thank*) was handed to me. Throughout the day I found countless things to be thankful for: small things like being able to wash my hair with only one hand, team-cook a nice meal with Hugo, and get out in the car to do a few errands—Hugo driving, of course. There were bigger things, too, like today's local paper dedicating a full page (with color photo) to Open Doors' Pets & Heroes event, held last November—and a non-profit theater group calling to see if Open Doors would be interested in accepting a donation from them!

Paul also talks about giving thanks in *all* circumstances, and that can be a challenge. But experience has proven that, no matter what comes our way, we can always find something to be thankful for. Tonight, one of those challenges confronted us—my older brother Howard, was rushed to the hospital with a massive heart attack. He actually died twice, but skilled and dedicated doctors revived him, working so vehemently that they broke a couple of his ribs in the process. What can I be thankful for now? How about the timing, treatment, and technology that have thus far kept him alive, his loving wife and family who now rally around him, the ardent prayers now going up on his behalf, the feeling that God is with us throughout all this, the closeness of loved ones who have gone before...?

Thanks for being very much with us at this difficult time, Lord,
watching over us, calming our fears with your promises,
and letting your Spirit intercede on our behalf, and Howard's behalf.

A kind, gentle man he is, a brother who sets a great example,
a loving, faithful family man, and strong believer--
a hard worker, brilliant, creative, cheerful, and caring.

Thanks for holding him close, cradling him in your loving arms.
You know what we want... we enjoy, need and love him so much!
You love him, too, so we release him to your care, now and always.

What About You?

1. What are you thankful for?

2. Dig deeper... How many grateful thoughts can you conjure up in the
   next sixty seconds?

3. When have you and others remembered/not remembered to say thank
   you? Who deserves and/or would appreciate a word of thanks right now?
   How can that be arranged?

Organize

January 10, 2010

Every New Year I resolve to get my house, time, projects—my entire life—better organized. It's on the list again this year. But this time I expect to make more headway because I'm more motivated (we hope to work our way to a warmer clime and want to travel light), and I'm better prepared, thanks to seeing some "eliminate clutter" techniques on TV and reading Peter Walsh's "It's All Too Much Stuff." And now that I have God's word on it, I'm inspired enough to get right to it. Last night I cleaned out the kitchen junk drawer, which I've ignored for years. Now I can open it easily and see exactly what's in there, all nicely organized. A drop in the bucket, yes... but a good start.

Paul told the new believers that all things should be done decently and in good order, even suggesting guidelines for their meetings and worship services. Jesus was less structured but certainly had his life in proper order, getting up early for some quiet time with his heavenly Father, and traveling light—not even a valise. His simple lifestyle let him focus completely on his mission, and gave him the flexibility to change his plans in an instant if something important unexpectedly came up. The Gospel of Mark tells how Jesus made time for blind Bartimaeus and so many others in desperate need. And when he and his disciples planned on getting away for some rest, the crowd got there first and begged for more time with him. Enough for that siesta! (See Mark 6.)

We can be more like Jesus and have things in proper order, too. He told us the secret! Seek first God and his kingdom, and all else will fall into place. (Matthew 6:33)

Heavenly Father, may the first thing I organize be my priorities.
I'll put you first, so I can see what and how to adjust my lifestyle:
what must go, what must increase, what must change.

When our hearts are turned toward you, we're in the best of hands:
you give us answers, set our courses, and provide for our needs.
Oh, how blessed we are!

This is the day you have made and I will rejoice and be glad in it.
Nature, perfectly ordered by you, sings your praises.
And I, a constant work in progress, sing your praises, too!

What About You?

1. What examples of good organization do you observe around you?

2. In what ways are you well (or not so well) organized?

3. What can you accomplish by drawing closer to God?

Listen

January 12, 2010

This word really hits home! I strongly suspect that I aggravate people by talking too much and listening too little. I know I do this because I recognize it myself and feel badly afterwards. I tend to say too much too soon, speaking before others can, and even cutting in when people are talking. I sometimes even anticipate what they're going to say and finish the thought for them—incorrectly, most of the time! I sure wish I could just be patient and quiet (two great virtues).

It's hard to believe I was once so shy I wouldn't open my mouth except in very familiar settings with very familiar people. People liked me better then, I think—before I was a big know-it-all. I don't know why I'm like this. Maybe I'm making up for all the times I wanted to say something but was afraid to speak out. Maybe it's also because I'm more passionate and enthusiastic about my beliefs and goals now, and forget to be self-conscious (until it's too late).

I definitely think God is giving me another loving hint—yes, we've recognized this problem many times and I'm still working on it. Perhaps this year, with God's help, I can make notable progress. Maybe I can apply the advice James gives in his epistle:

> Be quick to listen and slow to speak or get angry. God will bless you in everything you do if you listen and obey. (James 1:19, 25b)

I think of Psalm 46:10: "Be still and know that I am God."
I feel your presence, Lord, as I sit quietly, close my eyes, and wait...
I relax in your arms, relieved that I don't have to always be on the go.

In fact, I get the feeling that you prefer that I just sit and be with you.
Worries fade, fears subside, regrets are "has-beens."
I am yours and you are mine.

The more I listen to you the more I bask in the sunshine of your love,
I feel euphoric and well taken care of.
You open my ears and shut my mouth. Thank you, Lord.

What About You?

1. What is God saying to you right now? What do you learn when you take time to listen to your own heart?

2. How can we listen with more than just our ears?

3. Listening often implies a related action or heeding. What voices are calling out to be heard--in your life and/or in the world? Which of them are you (and which should you be) listening to?

Wait

January 15, 2010

Isaiah 40:31 says that those who wait on the Lord have strength and endurance. *Wait* is a difficult word for me. It has a double edge to it because I'm impetuous and hasty in order to avoid having to wait, yet I keep others waiting. I rush around (which is dangerous and unhealthy) and end up displeased with the outcome or rudely late. Even my dog, Jessie, knows not to get too excited when I announce a walk, because the wait between the announcement and the walk can stretch on as I do "just this" and "just that." I've wrestled with both sides of the problem (not wanting to wait, yet making others wait) for a long time without sufficient progress. Just tonight I busied myself until it was time for a church dinner—and still had to dress for it.

Rudyard Kipling's poem "If" talks about what it takes to attain maturity and wisdom, and one phrase comes to mind: *If you can wait and not be tired by waiting...* It's time for me to finally learn to be patient and wait rather than rush in where angels fear to tread. I also have to respect others' time by not making them wait. I can start already tonight by not aggravating Hugo by getting to bed late—and tomorrow, Sunday, I can leave for church in plenty of time instead of cutting it frighteningly close or ending up late again. Our new pastor will preach for the first time tomorrow morning—how awful if I'm late for that!

I also have to exert some patience when it comes to investing in a Florida property. We're finally getting out of a bad investment we made in Las Vega (due to my impulsiveness and refusal to hear the promptings and wise counsel given at that time). I think previous words: *listen, relax, pray,* and *envision* can help to guide me in deciding about a place near our loved ones in Florida.

Those who wait on the Lord will have strength and endurance (Is 40:31).
I can do it! I can learn to wait by waiting on you, Lord.
I will wait for you to direct me one way or another.

I will slow down, be more careful, listen more intently.
I will plan my time and activities so I don't insult others by being late.
I can't do it on my own—but with your help I can.

Right now, this very moment, I make a covenant with you—
to stay in constant touch with you so I can feel your promptings
and go in the right direction. Thank you, Lord. All praise be yours.

What About You?

1. When are you most impatient? How has that been a problem?

2. When has patience paid off for you or someone else?

3. What covenant or promise can you make that will help to make
    waiting easier?

Weep

January 18, 2010

It's OK to cry—Jesus, did. When his friend, Lazarus, died, Jesus tar-ried, so rather than healing him he did something even more spectacular: he raised his friend from the dead. And even though he knew the outcome of his visit with Mary and Martha (Lazarus' sisters), he couldn't help but share in their grief. We are told in the Gospel of John that *he wept*.

At my friend's memorial service yesterday a recent widow who was attending just cried and cried. She apologized profusely. I hope I com-forted her a bit by reminding her that crying, in her position, is good and therapeutic—that's why God gave us tears. I also gave her some practical assistance by supplying some tissues.

Later that evening tears filled my eyes as I watched a segment of Oprah that interviewed people who'd lost love ones in an auto accident that was caused by someone texting on his cell phone while driving. Also interviewed was the young man whose texting caused the accident. So much pain…

Then, as I watched the news, tears again stung my eyes as I saw the devastation caused by the earthquake in Haiti. Sometimes there's nothing we can do *but cry*. But in this case there is plenty that needs to be done to locate and bury the dead and help the survivors. It's heartwarming to see the great outreach from all over the world to help this poor country deal with this massive tragedy.

Thank you, Lord, for crying with us, as Jesus did with Mary and Martha.
May we, like Jesus, couple our tears with helpful actions.
Please guide and bless those in need and those who help.

I pray for wisdom, discernment, humility, understanding and compassion.
It's easier to look the other way because caring deeply is so very painful.
But by sharing others' burdens we reflect your love, don't we, Lord?

It's so overwhelming when we think of the pain in the world.
Thanks for promising that one day there will be no more tears.
Peace and love will win out--and we'll finally meet Jesus face to face.

What About You?

1. When have others helped to dry your tears—and you, theirs?

2. What heartfelt pain (your own or someone else's) are you presently feeling? How are you dealing with it?

3. When and how has the Lord helped you/others during difficult times? How can you lean on God now?

Rejoice

January 20, 2010

It's a totally sunny, mild day here in New Jersey—a real mid-winter treat! My broken wrist is healing well and my bone density test shows no osteoporosis. My brother, Howard, has made a miraculous turn for the better after his massive heart attack. Hugo's root canal and sinus infection will soon be a thing of the past. And best of all, I feel closer to the Lord as, day by day, I listen, follow, and apply one word at a time.

Yes, I have many good reasons to rejoice, so I'm delighted with today's word (which came to me as I was out walking my dog, Jessie—another blessing I rejoice over.) And we can't leave out Annabelle, our cat who loves Jessie so much. I wish we could all get along as well as they do. Which leads me to an even greater rejoicing—over our three-month old granddaughter, Jessica Ruth, who just had her first laughing spree. Nothing could stop her, and all the people around her couldn't help but join right in. Maybe a little angel told her the word of the day, and she rejoiced *with* me!

How can we rejoice, you may ask, when there is such pain and heartache all around us—and perhaps even in our own family? Maybe *we ourselves* are in the "pits" because of present circumstances. No matter how bad things are, we can always find things to rejoice over if we just look for them. This type of rejoicing does us a world of good, inspiring and strengthening us to meet whatever challenges lie before us.

In Mt 5:3-12 Jesus encourages the grieving, the meek, the disheartened...
by reminding them that God has good things in store for them.
He even tells those who are persecuted to be glad and rejoice.

You, Lord, are our greatest reason to rejoice.
Because of you our lives have meaning, power, and joy.
And we know that with you all things are possible!

Weeping may endure for a night, but joy comes in the morning (Ps 30:5).
How comforting it is to know that with you our future is bright.
Meanwhile may peace, contentment, and faith be our stronghold.

What About You?

1. What past joys still light up your life and warm your heart each time you think of them?

2. What are you happy about today? How many things can you list?

3. Paul says to rejoice in the Lord who has planned wonderfully unimaginable things for those who love him (Phil 4:4, 1 Co 2:9). What other joy-producing Scriptures or thoughts come to mind?

Enjoy

January 21, 2010

This is one of my favorite words! Why? Because enjoyment can be a gift we give to others as well as ourselves. I have a bookmark that says: *Those who bring sunshine into the lives of others cannot keep it from themselves.* One of the best things we can do for people, especially children, is to just enjoy them. It's a secret to a happy marriage, too! Ecclesiastes 9:9 says: *Life is short, so enjoy being with your spouse. This is what you are supposed to do as you struggle through life on this earth.* In Paul's first letter to Timothy he talks about God supplying us with all things to enjoy—things money can't buy. In fact, money often makes it harder to see and enjoy the best life has to offer. St. Francis "hit the nail on the head" when he said: *The way to happiness is not by adding to our possessions, but by subtracting from our wants.*

Just look around—and within. There's so much to enjoy in life! Rather than worrying about the past or fretting about the future, we are far better off to be content right now, in the present—enjoying what we have. I love being retired and able to work at home, doing what I feel called to do. I can now more fully use the talents, and pursue the interests, God gave me. I'm so grateful that I can run my own non-profit foundation and do things my way, making it fun as well as helpful. And I'm thankful that I can finally have a dog again, after 45 years without one—and I can really enjoy her because I'm not on a rigid work schedule anymore. And, most of all, I love being able to relax and enjoy my unique relationship with God, letting it ebb and flow, trying new things, and being ready to go in whatever direction God may send me.

This is the day the Lord has made; I'll make the most of it.
I'll enjoy the marvels of nature—the sun, the moon, the stars,
the life around me: plants, animals and especially the people!

Also the food, the music, the softness of Annabelle the cat's velvety coat...
good health, the new pastor to lead and inspire our church family...
drawing closer to our daughter and family in Florida and to you, Lord!

Photographs, happy memories, long-time friends and new acquaintances,
things to learn, places to go, projects to take part in...
and You, who are love, forgiveness, perfection—the joy of my life.

What About You?

1. What do you enjoy most?

2. What areas of your life lack enjoyment? How can you make them more enjoyable?

3. What are some ways to enjoy others? To enjoy God?

Beware

January 24, 2010

Who's afraid of the big, bad wolf? Not me—unless he comes knocking at *my* door! Talk is cheap till you've walked the walk. I know that I tend to take people's pain, grief, and fear too lightly and not adequately help them. And I'm certainly aware that I also tend to maintain too casual an attitude toward the Almighty, forgetting what an all-powerful force he actually is—worthy of stand-back reverence and knee-bending adoration, not just buddy-buddy friendship. So I guess you could say that "beware" to me starts with *beware* of feeling too much in control of God and *beware* of trivializing people's deepest emotions.

On a lighter but relevant note, I must also beware of reversing good decisions--like today, when I retrieved (and gobbled up) the half-bag of M&M's I threw in the garbage last night. The last thing I should be eating is candy, especially not in large quantities like 14 ounces in two sittings. Nowadays we must beware of letting food (drugs, smoking, alcohol, sex, etc.) take the place of the real Comforter, the Holy Spirit, and *beware* of giving in to short-term pleasures that sabotage long-lasting peace, joy, wholeness, and health.

Jesus said, *Beware of false prophets, who come to you in sheep's clothing, but inwardly are ravening wolves. (Mt 7:15)* In our contemporary world it means steering clear of offers that are too good to be true (like many of those TV infomercials I succumb to!)... people who have hidden agendas (like some of those marketers that call at dinnertime)... and "friends" who offer drugs and/or suggest things that are definitely not in our best interest.

Jesus said to beware of the Scribes and Pharisees, "slick" know-it-alls
who are inwardly mean and selfish. Anyone like that in today's world?
Peter says to run from the devil, a roaring lion out to devour us.

James says to resist the devil and he will flee from us. The mother
of Walter Cronkite advised him to avoid anything questionable…
and he was known as a man of high integrity throughout his news career.

I aim to beware of small compromises that can grow into huge problems,
haughty attitudes that can place pride between me and thee, Lord,
and careless words that can never be recalled.

What About You?

1. What does the word beware say to you?

2. What examples can you think of that illustrate some subtle things that we should watch out for?

3. What questionable-type things do you think Mrs. Cronkite had in mind when she gave that advice? What wisdom and good advice can you pass on to others, based on your wisdom and experience?

Create

January 26, 2010

This morning, while reading Martha Grace Reese's book, "Unbinding Your Heart," this sentence jumped out at me: *God loves creation. God made us, the animals, our beautiful earth.* It reminds me that I, too, love creation—and *creating*! As a child, I wrote a poem about mosquitoes buzzing around my head as I tried to sleep (no air conditioning in those days). At age nine I wrote a poem, which I still have, called "I Wonder:" *Always when I look up high I wonder what is in the sky...* As a pre-teen I enjoyed writing little stories and plays. As an adult I wrote newsletters, customized shows for children at school and church, and two books— one for teachers and one written in the voice of my dog. Still today, I like to create something totally unique that wasn't there before and will only get done if *I* do it.

I always loved music, too! My mother gave me a little plastic record for my fourth birthday, and I played it again and again on our Victrola. It had catchy songs like "A Frog Went A'Courting," "Oh, Dear, What Can the Matter Be," and "All Around the Cobbler's Bench." A few years later, I pestered an older girl in our neighborhood to sing "Red River Valley" umpteen times in a row. I also pestered to play a musical instrument, and had wonderful times playing the saxophone. Of course I loved hymns and the Young Life songs, which I still sing. In my fifties I received a *marvelous* blessing: I woke up early one morning with a message from God—in the form of a song. I jumped up and jotted down the five verses and main chorus:

> *Time with me, time with me...beloved child, spend some time with me.*
> *I love you so, but there's no way you'll know unless you spend a little time with me.*

Thanks, Lord, for being so creative, and for making us in your image.
When you surveyed your workmanship you called it good.
The more we learn the more we're amazed and say "Awesome!"

When we're facing a problem you say: Create some possible solutions.
When we're stressed, you say: Create a place for me in your life.
When we're bored or lazy, you say: Create a plan and get going.

I feel your satisfaction as you say to Isaiah: Behold, I will do a new thing.
and when Paul writes: If anyone is in Christ, s/he is a new creation!
and when John talks of a new heaven and a new earth (Rev 21:1).

What About You?

1. What do you find most amazing about God's creation?

2. What will you leave behind that wouldn't have happened or been here without your participation in life?

3. How do you plan to use your talents and interests right now and/or in the future?

Appreciate

January 31, 2010

Wow! We have so much to appreciate in our lives, and so often we take it all for granted—until we lose part of our blessings. I for one can say that by breaking my wrist I now have a greater appreciation for our hands and how wonderfully they serve us.

I often remind myself to be more appreciative of my wonderful husband. He's been very faithful, loving, and helpful over the forty-two years we've been together. I owe so much to him, and I want to lovingly consider his needs and desires as I forge ahead on my own projects. He's turning 81 this May and I want his later years to be content and productive, and I know that my actions can make a big difference in the quality of his life during these coming years.

I also appreciate our country and the freedoms we enjoy, thanks to the sacrifices of so many. Just last week a young man from the neighboring town died in Iraq. Thousands came out to honor him as his casket made its way through the center of town to the church and on to the cemetery. We Americans today have so much—even *too* much. We build bigger houses and buy more things, but too much somehow makes us less appreciative.

Finally, I appreciate our religious freedom—being able to worship and serve God in our own individual ways. Some people believe they serve God when they hurt innocent people. We do not understand that, for we serve a *loving* God who wills that none should perish, and wants us to appreciate the fact that he loves each and every one of us.

We get up each day and do our own thing—praise the Lord!
We drive cars, read books, and eat healthy food—praise the Lord!
We vote, speak our minds, and go on vacations—praise the Lord!

We have Bibles in all versions and translations—hurray!
We start businesses and set up charities to help others—hurray!
We try new things and dream big dreams—hurray!

We appreciate you, Lord, for your goodness and mercy.
We appreciate you, Jesus, and your great love for us.
We appreciate you, Holy Spirit, for connecting us to God and Jesus.

What About You?

1.   What do you appreciate most?

2.   What are some ways in which we can show our appreciation? Which do you think are most pleasing to God? Why?

3.   How can we help others to be more appreciative?

Work

February 1, 2010

In Paul's second letter to his young assistant, Timothy, he instructs Timothy to do his best to win God's approval as a worker who doesn't need to be ashamed. That's the kind of worker I want to be: honest, diligent, reliable, productive...

Of all the Proverbs that mention the word *lazy* I like 20:4 the best: *If you're too lazy to plow, don't expect a harvest.* Solomon also says, *Work hard and you will be a leader* and *Hard work is worthwhile.* So I will continue to work hard and do my best, and try to do as Paul told the people in Corinth: *Do everything to the glory of God.*

Remember some of the good old sayings and rhymes that were motivating and inspiring? Ones like, "If at first you don't succeed, try, try again!" and:

> *Good, better, best*
> *Never let it rest*
> *Till the good is better*
> *And the better best.*

Jesus worked hard teaching, healing, and holding his own against his adversaries. By the end of the day he was exhausted. The Bible tells how, when he and his disciples tried to sail across the lake to rest, the crowd ran around the lake and was there waiting when they came to shore (See Mark 6:30-44). What did Jesus *do*? Instead of resting he continued to teach, heal, and even put his disciples to work feeding the thousands of people!

Doctors, nurses, rescue workers and others are right now in Haiti,
helping those in such dire need after a killer earthquake.
People from around the world are sending food and clothing to them.

"The harvest is plentiful," Jesus says, "but the workers are few." (Mt 9:37)
He also told his followers to go and tell the Good News. (Mk 16:15)
And because of many tireless workers we are believers today.

Now it's our turn: "To whom much is given, much is required." (Lk 12:48)
We must work like it depends on us and pray like it depends on God.
In time Jesus will say to us, "Well done, good and faithful servant."

What About You?

1. How much do you think God expects us to do?

2. What would you like your obituary to say about you?

3. What task has been calling your name? Is it time to respond?

Sing

February 2, 2010

What a marvelous gift we've all been given—the ability to sing. Obviously, some of us are more talented than others, but we can all make a joyful noise—by singing, humming, whistling, and/or playing musical instruments. And those of us blessed with good hearing can enjoy music by *listening* and letting the words and melodies speak to our hearts.

David and the other psalmists have given us that wonderful Book of Psalms: *songs* meant to be sung, shared, and used to inspire us and praise the Lord. When our pastor asked each of the people in our study group to identify his/her favorite book of the Bible, the Psalms won out, hands over. Most of those who chose the Psalms are judging them on the words alone. Can you imagine their power when put to music and sung with combined voices? *I will sing to the LORD as long as I live; I will sing praise to my God while I have my being.* (104:33)

The writer of the book of James says that if we're in trouble we should pray, and if we're feeling good we should sing praises. Today, as Jessie my dog and I walked in the woods along the river by our house, I sang songs of praise—ones I haven't sung in a long time. I didn't have to worry about impressing or aggravating or scaring anyone—I could just sing to the Lord with all my heart. The deer took off immediately, but Jessie enjoyed it! (She is, however, a bit hard of hearing.)

Songs can work wonders when we're feeling badly, too.
If we sing despite our misery, what a difference it can make.
Thank you, Lord, for songs and singers, music and musicians.

Paul told the people at the church of Ephesus: "Sing psalms, hymns and
spiritual songs, as you praise the Lord with all your heart."
Jesus sang, too—before facing betrayal and death (Mark 14).

No wonder you have chosen this word for us today, dear Lord,
for when we lift our voices in song we lift our hearts to you
and sing in the company of angels!

What About You?

1. What songs have touched *your* heart?

2. What would life be like *without* music?

3. I have many happy memories of strumming the guitar and singing— a skill I learned at an adult evening-school class. What difference has music made in *your* life?

Improve

February 13, 2010

There's always a big run on the "new and improved" version of a product, and just imagine how much is spent each year by people wanting to look, feel, and do better. Come to think of it, even the purpose of this word-a-day project is to improve—that's why, thus far, I think the best title for what we're doing is *Come, Grow with Me*. You, dear readers, are watching me strive to improve as I ponder and write about an action verb that's inspired, I believe, by God. Each entry ends with some questions so you, too, can strive to improve, each in your own unique way.

We just have to be careful when it comes to improving others. Jesus said to check out the "board" in our own eyes before trying to remove the "splinter" in someone else's. (Mt 7:3-5) I now see that I'm facing the wrong way when I tell my daughter and son-in-law what to do and not to do--I'm actually turning my back on what Jesus said. From now on I'll stay out of their business as much as I can and just enjoy and encourage them. When I falter I'll recall the only line I often quote from my college course in Shakespeare: *"Striving to better, oft we mar what's well."* (*King Lear, Act 1, Scene 4*)

Even self-improvement is tricky--we have to watch not to overdo it. As a new mother I was very determined to do it right. I read lots of books on parenting, and each one inspired me to make the suggested changes. One highly respected "expert" recommended disciplining by hitting your child on the hand with a wooden spoon—that turned out to be one of my biggest regrets. I now advocate no hitting or spanking. Throughout our daughter's growing years I kept so-called "improving" and we ended up with a rebellious teen who accused me of being much too inconsistent. And she was right—I was so busy improving, I actually made things worse.

I've a ways to go when it comes to this word, Lord.
  The key is to listen to the right expert,
    and there's only one expert who really knows what's best–you!

We must turn to you as those who lived in Jesus' day turned to him.
  We need healing (both physical and spiritual) and words of hope.
    We need peace, a purpose, and a Friend who sees our potential.

We're not here to strive for perfection or to satisfy our ambitions.
  We're here to enjoy life, help others, and serve you.
    What better way is there to improve and be the best we can be?

What About You?

1. What or who do you think needs improving? What can/should you do about it?

2. Do you have, or know of, an improvement story with a surprise ending?

3. How can you and God team up to make important and far-reaching improvements?

Harmonize

February 14, 2010

What a joy it is to hear musical harmony—it lifts, relaxes, inspires. I still recall how beautifully the voices of the Lennon sisters blended together when they sang on the Lawrence Welk Show so many years ago. And among my happiest memories are the times when my dad would take out his old C-Melody saxophone and transpose so we could play the duets written for my E-Flat sax. I was just a kid learning the sax, but the harmonies we produced together still echo in my heart.

Many people prefer to have the melody (the lead) in life's "songs." But, harmonizing with the lead melody is also very gratifying. Nobody wants to play second fiddle in a relationship, but the second violins in the orchestra add a depth, a fullness, and an enriching beauty to the melody line. I'm not the greatest singer, but I much prefer to sing alto when the song is right and I can handle it. I'd love to be able to sing well enough to perform with the Sweet Adelines or some other singing group. Meanwhile I'll work at being a different type of harmonizer…

I may never travel the world to promote peace and understanding, but I can be a peacemaker right here where I am. In his Beatitudes, Jesus promises that peacemakers will be blessed, happy, and rewarded by being called children of God. How I wish I could go back and sow harmony where I've sown discord and hurt feelings. I've heard it said that hell is when we get to see the full extent of the pain we've caused others. We can't erase our past, but thanks to Jesus' harmonizing work on the cross, we're forgiven and can do better in the future.

It's truly wonderful when relatives live together in peace (Ps 133:1).
What a difference we can make when we're at-home harmonizers!
Our every thought, word, and action can make things better.

Paul says (Ro 12) to share joys and sorrows, give to those in need,
honor others above selves, and strive for peace with everyone.
In other words, to harmonize whenever and however possible!

Jesus promises a very special inner peace that only he can give.
It quells worry and fear, and fills us with a wellspring of harmony
from which we can draw in the best of times and the worst of times.

What About You?

1. What are some of your favorite examples of musical or other types of harmony?

2. When have you, or someone you know, overcome evil with good by injecting some skillful harmonizing?

3. What situations need a good dose of harmony? How can you/we be a part of the solution?

Prepare

February 15, 2010

Both *plan* and *prepare* have been floating around in my psyche the last twenty-four hours. I'm going to go with *prepare* because I've already *planned* to do the book launch, de-clutter the house, simplify my life, and vacation next week in Florida. *Now* I have to do the preparations for these (and other) diverse, challenging, and enjoyable plans I've made. Planning is like saying you're going to do something, while preparing is actually *doing* something to move it along. [Time out: We're getting our valises out for our upcoming trip.] Now, *that's* preparing!

I'm a dyed-in-the-wool coward. I've had an exceptionally easy and blessed life, but I know that into each life varying degrees of heartache and pain must come. And to all, death will come. So, most of my life I've been preparing by gathering as much spiritual strength as I can so, when tough times *do* come, I'll be on a first-name basis with the only One who can truly help me.

And, you know what? I've already had some tough times—but with God's help I've come through them stronger than before. I recall begging God to answer my fervent prayer, and was blessed with an ounce of prevention (a vision to cling to), a pound of first aid (Scriptures to ward off negative thoughts), and a ton of long-term assurance that the Spirit is with me at all times.

My lifelong preparation had already paid off! I was not alone during the worst of times. And my good Friend, who stayed with me throughout, is still with me now and will hold my hand as I slip (or stumble) from this life into the next.

38

The shock waves came, when least expected—a virtual tsunami of trauma.
I walked around like a zombie. Did people notice I was different?
I couldn't eat—or pray. Thankfully, the Spirit took over for me.

Friends and loved ones prayed, not knowing why I wanted them to.
As I was shaking in bed, I felt myself raised up, surrounded by prayer.
Scriptures I knew (and forgot I knew) stood guard and calmed me.

Whenever a fearful thought assaulted me, a comforting Word superseded it.
Soon I had pages filled with powerful and inspiring promises.
Years have passed; the crisis has subsided…and still I prepare!

What About You?

1. What do you think are the best ways to prepare for the unexpected in life?

2. What can you do right now to prepare for a richer, fuller, more spiritual life?

3. What Scriptures do you know by heart? List them and keep adding to the list!

Accept

February 16, 2010

This word ended up making a lot of sense today. It started with a lovely winter snow, something like 4 to 6 inches. It wasn't heavy and aggressive, but soft and willowy, clinging to the branches and painting a gorgeous scene for all to enjoy. (It was easy for us to accept it since we didn't have to drive in the rush hour!) We did venture out to the doctor's in the afternoon to finally get the cast taken off my wrist. My broken wrist was not so easy to accept, but once broken, acceptance was the only way to go. Now I must accept the agony of physical therapy!

Today we called our friends, Andy and Gladdy. They're such fun to talk with--always full of fascinating insights and wise advice. I so often resist advice and make it difficult for anyone wanting to help me. Could God have sent me today's word to remind me that I'm a know-it-all who knows so little? Sometimes we all need to listen and heed others' experience and wisdom. Hugo still thinks I'm taking on too many smaller tasks that take my time and concentration from the bigger tasks that will reach more people. I accept that he's got a good point there, but I somehow keep accepting more tasks that he considers to be small—like helping my friend's sister (visiting from Thailand) to learn more English, and organizing a sing-along for my developmentally-challenged friends.

I think I need to ponder that well-known saying, attributed to both St. Francis and Reinhold Niebuhr, the one used constantly by twelve-step groups like Alcoholics Anonymous:

> *Lord, grant me the serenity to accept the things I cannot change; the courage to change the things that I can; and the wisdom to know the difference.*

40

Grant me discernment, Lord, so I can see things as they truly are.
Help me know what to accept and what to change, especially in myself.
Then please help me to make the necessary changes!

As a Christian, I accept human limitations; we can only do so much.
Help me to be selective—to choose those things that you value.
Let me drop those things that don't bring us closer to you.

As a Christian, I accept the finished work of Jesus Christ on the cross,
the free gifts you give us: life, love, forgiveness, and an eternity with you.
I also accept, and wholeheartedly do, whatever tasks you send my way.

What About You?

1. Is there anything in your life that you haven't yet accepted, that perhaps you should?

2. Whose advice and information are you most likely to accept? Who looks to you for that type of help?

3. Jesus said we should be like children, open and accepting of his truths. Is there anything in the Christian faith that you find hard to accept? What can you do about it?

Aim

February 17, 2010

Today is Ash Wednesday, the start of Lent. Ashes on the forehead symbolize our penitence, for we are weak, dependent, and, yes, sinful. The aim of the 40 days of Lent (symbolic of Jesus' 40 days in the wilderness) is to prepare us for Holy Week and Easter—through prayer, study, worship, and self-denial. It is customary to give up something in honor of the Lord who sacrificed his son for us. My aim this Lent is to give up three things: something for God, something for others, and something for my own good. So I'm giving up being late to church, interrupting people as they speak, and chocolate. Actually all three will serve me well, proving that the more we do for God and others the more we are blessed.

When Jesus was in the wilderness he was preparing for his divine ministry—and he knew exactly what he was aiming for: God's will. When Satan tempted him three times he kept his focus and was victorious. We, too, must aim high—shoot for the stars! Of course we're not perfect as Jesus was, so we'll fall short--but maybe we'll at least hit the "moon."

St. Paul told his church at Philippi that he takes aim and runs toward the goal: heaven. He says, *This is the prize God offers because of what Jesus has done. (Phil 3:14)* And even though Paul met with all kinds of undeserved punishment and overwhelming challenges while telling the Good News and starting the first Christian churches, he was content and filled with joy. *Rejoice!* he said, *Again I say, rejoice!* Aiming high helps to ward off selfishness, succumbing to temptation, and making all sorts of foolish decisions—it also makes us happy. *(Phil 3:14)*

42

Ask 3 different masons what they're doing. One says, "Laying bricks."
Another: "Making a wall." The third: "Building a cathedral."
Help us to look up, Lord, and set our sights on the big picture.

The best way to make a straight furrow is to look ahead, not down.
Aim for a tree or other object, and the path will be straight.
Help us to aim for, and attain, our highest and noblest goals.

When we know where we're headed our lives have meaning and value.
We're no longer shortsighted; we don't sweat the small stuff.
Help us to find favor in your sight, Lord, as we go in your direction.

What About You?

1. In what direction is your life aiming? Are you pleased with it?

2. What are your noblest goals? Are you aiming toward them as you live each day?

3. What are some good ways to help others set their sights in God's direction?

43

Practice

The saying "Practice makes perfect" is a bit of an exaggeration, but the well-practiced Olympic performances this past week in Canada come mighty close to perfection. I recall being a seventh-grade saxophone player in the junior high school band and having a tricky lead-in to our part in "Light Cavalry." I knew it was a stumbling block, so I put in extra time and effort to practice it, and my efforts paid off. The perfectionist band leader caught our sloppy entry and asked each of us sax players to play it in front of the whole band—talk about pressure! Because I was the only one that played it correctly I went from 5th seat to first seat in an instant.

In mid-life I took a course in contemplative prayer, given by our wonderful pastor at that time. I was so touched by it that I continued the practice on my own after the course ended. The more I practiced, the closer I got to the Lord—it was very powerful and even a little scary to draw so close. I later joined the Network of Biblical Storytellers and did a lot of practicing to learn the Books of Mark, Jonah, and James by heart—as well as the fruit of the Spirit, the Love Chapter, and Psalm 139. Just recently, as a senior citizen, I wanted to re-learn Psalm 139 and, because of my earlier practice, I was able to recapture it fully in less than a half hour.

I'm 66 and Hugo almost 81, yet we strive to maintain our love-life, something highly recommended for physical and psychological reasons. It doesn't always work out as we'd like, but when it doesn't, we're just as happy because it just means that we need more practice!

Jesus sent the disciples in pairs to try telling the Good News.
Doctors practice the art of medicine; their learning never stops.
People devotedly practice music, sports, and other passions.

Through practice we nurture the Spirit's fruit: peace, goodness, love,
joy, kindness, gentleness, faithfulness, patience, and self control.
Prayer, Bible-reading, and worship keep us well-oiled.

I need to practice letting go of my controlling spirit...writing
New Year's resolutions for loved ones is way too controlling!
I'll practice listening, caring, and telling God's Good News.

What About You?

1. Do you have any real-life "Practice makes better" stories?

2. Where do you need to invest more time and effort?

3. Which fruit of the Spirit jumps out at you? Why do you think that is?

Renew

February 19, 2010

We renew lots of things: magazine subscriptions, memberships to all manner of associations, and even our cars' registrations. Right now (seven weeks after breaking my wrist) I'm working on a form of renewal; I'm doing what it takes to get my left side fully functioning again. I had my first physical therapy session today, and I see that it will be a slow and painful process, but I'm committed to it.

Fortunately all renewals aren't so painful. Hugo and I were very happy to renew our wedding vows—twice. During the third ceremony tears filled his eyes (something I rarely see in my stalwart husband!) I treasure those tears because they reveal the depth of the love we share together—a love that we will lean on as we grow older together. In a way, we already started doing this these past seven weeks as Hugo did what I could no longer do for myself. He buttoned, zipped, cut, drove, and did all manner of things—to compensate for my healing wrist.

Martin Luther tended toward depression but he was always able to counteract it by another form of renewal. Whenever he recalled his baptism, it turned things around for him and enabled him to start anew. In Psalms, David prayed earnestly for the renewal of a right spirit so that his relationship with God would be restored and the sins that plagued him would be forgiven. Thus, in David's case, it was repentance and confession that precipitated his much-desired renewal.

Mark 1:15 says that Jesus started his ministry by saying: "God's kingdom will soon be here. Turn back to God and believe the Good News." He says the same thing to us today.

Paul told the Romans (12:2) to renew their minds and think about what is pure, right, holy, friendly, proper, worthwhile, worthy of praise. Both Paul and Jesus (see Matt. 5:28) saw the power of our minds!

Revelation 2:5a tells of Ephesians who drifted from their good start. "Think back... and then do as you did at first." Turning and returning to Jesus is always the way to go!

What About You?

1. What needs to be renewed in *your* life?

2. What memories do you have of God working in your life that can be helpful during difficult times?

3. Which of the renewals mentioned resonate most with you? Why?

Spread

February 23, 2010

We put a spread on our bread to enhance the taste;
we put a spread on the bed to protect and beautify;
we spread "sunshine" and good will to increase the world's joy;
we spread the Good News to give meaning and hope to life.

Jesus commissioned his followers to go throughout the world and spread the Word. They waited faithfully for the Holy Spirit to come and spread among them the power they needed to fulfill the command. The tongues of fire produced all sorts of miracles as our spiritual forebears stepped out in faith. Peter's first sermon drew in 3,000 new believers--and the words he spoke reached the ears of the listeners in whatever language they understood. (See Acts, chapter 2.)

As we read the Book of Acts we get a first-hand account of what it took to spread the Good News in a world as full of pain and hostility as ours is today. We see Peter healing people, being arrested and beaten, yet refusing to stop talking about Jesus when ordered to do so. We watch as angels miraculously free him from jail to continue his mission.

How thrilling it is to see Saul (persecutor of Christians) changed into Paul (spreader of churches and writer of powerful letters) through a dramatic encounter with the risen Christ. We also witness him and Silas being beaten and jailed, yet singing God's praises and voluntarily remaining in jail even though they can easily escape (thus impressing and converting the jailer!)

Make me a spreader, Lord…
   using my time for the tasks that call my name,
      until I drop all else to focus on that one special project.

Make me a spreader, Lord…
   sharing my money with needy people and worthwhile causes,
      until I put it all into one "pearl of great price." (Mt 13:44-46)

Make me a spreader, Lord…
   giving love to the unlovable as well as the lovable,
      until you wrap undeserving me in your loving arms and call me home.

What About You?

1.   What types of *spreading* are you now involved in?

2.   What are some ways we can answer God's call to spread his Good News far and wide?

3.   How have various people (and God) spread goodness in your life?

Move

February 25, 2010

Boy! Did I ever move this morning—as I chased the hat that blew off my head right into the Gulf of Mexico! Here I was taking a nice relaxing walk on the beach as our week in Florida was drawing to a close, and before I knew it I was standing in the Gulf catching my floating hat on a returning wave—surely a dramatic way to start my thought processes going in the direction of our word for the day. My wet socks, shoes, and rescued hat were appropriate trophies for a quick response to an urgent situation.

I sure wish I'd been as responsive to some much more important situations in my past. I regret terribly not reacting quickly enough to warn a car *not* go down the one-way ramp it was entering. As I stood waiting to cross the ramp, the car started down. It took me a few seconds to process the situation and then it was too late. What a helpless, guilty feeling I harbored as sirens blared and I prayed for minimal damage, asking God to do what was now out of my hands. If only I had responded as automatically as I did today on the beach—I would have tried to flag the car down, shouted for all I was worth, even stood in front of the car if possible.

Another time Hugo and I were at a local restaurant dining with our friend, Mike, when a woman started choking on her food and her companion shouted for help. I froze, but thank heaven, Mike jumped right up, gave the Heimlich maneuver, and saved the woman's life. How I admire him for moving so quickly and decisively without giving it a second thought!

May I always move in ways that help others and honor you, Lord:
sharing joys and sorrows, lending a hand or a shoulder to lean on
as I forget about myself and follow you.

Help me to move, dear Jesus, as you moved when you were here:
toward places of quiet for refreshment and communion with God,
toward those who need a healing touch or words of wisdom and hope.

Help me to move, dear Spirit, when you tell me to,
then I'll also know when not to speak or act, which is equally important.
And I'll know if and when to move to Florida…

What About You?

1. How has God been moving in *your* life?

2. What moves have you made that you're proud of? Which actions or inactions have you regretted?

3. What moves are your presently contemplating? Have you asked God's help in deciding the when, where, and how of those moves?

Believe

February 28, 2010

It's a matter of choice. We either believe or we don't. We can easily *say* we believe, but if we truly believe we will act on it. For example, if someone shouts "Fire!" we first *decide* if we'll believe it. If we choose to believe it, then we move—*quickly*—to save ourselves and others. The Book of James, chapter two, says this (and more) about faith:

> What good is it to say you have faith, when you don't do anything to show that you really do have faith?.. Faith that doesn't lead us to do good deeds is all alone and dead!... Suppose someone disagrees and says, "It is possible to have faith without doing kind deeds." I would answer, "Prove that you have faith without doing kind deeds, and I will prove that I have faith by doing them.

Obviously, the truth of what we're believing does not lie in *our* hands. For example, the person shouting "Fire!" may just be "crying wolf." We can't be sure of exactly how God will bring his promises to fruition, but the more we step out in faith with our good deeds, the more our faith and trust is confirmed. Chapter 11 in the Book of Hebrews tells us about the great faith of so many of our spiritual ancestors, and says: *Faith is the substance of things hoped for and the evidence of things not seen.* It is what propels us to live in a way that honors God and others, because we *know in our hearts* that God's promises are sure. We just need to take a look at the natural world (and our amazing minds and bodies) to get more than enough evidence to solidify our faith in the One who made and controls it all.

*"How can God let so much bad happen if he's in control?" people ask.
I find consolation in Jesus' story about letting the plants and weeds (the
good and bad) grow together until harvest time. [See Mt 13:24-43.]*

*I find comfort in believing that God weeps with us when tragedy comes,
sees us through, and holds our hands as we face the insurmountable.
All outcomes are in his hands, and the final outcome will be good.*

*I believe in a God who knows us at our worst—and loves us still;
who knows our names and is there for us when we call his name;
who forgives, chastises, and delights in us as much as we delight in him.*

What About You?

1. What are *your* basic beliefs about God and his promises?

2. What great people of faith have touched your life?

3. What gives you comfort when you see and feel the many problems in
   our world today? How can we, as believers, make a positive
   difference?

Teach

March 2, 2010

Going to school was something very special for me, a four-year-old with no preschool experience. In my day, girls wore dresses and skirts (no jeans, even for the boys) and teachers wore suits/dresses. In school I was a totally different person (quiet and shy!) There were 30-some-odd children per elementary teacher--with very few discipline problems. We were all pretty much in awe of this amazing experience. I can still recall my first day of kindergarten—rushing home (we lived right across the street from the school) to tell Mom how wonderful it was.

Having an older brother and sister helped. I'd watch them going off to school and wonder why I couldn't go. My sister (one school year ahead of me) would teach me songs she'd learned at school and my brother (four school years ahead of me) taught me fractions and even algebra way ahead of my time. I remember being so anxious to write, I'd fill a lined paper with row-upon-row of wavy lines which, held at arms length, looked very much like writing to *me*!

As a teenager I earned 50-cents an hour babysitting. I also earned money as a Latin tutor in junior high school and a remedial reading tutor as a college freshman. And during college I worked summers as a playground director, so it's not surprising that I became a teacher. I aspired to be a veterinarian, but I ended up at a state teacher's college. I was hesitant going in, but by the end of freshman year the classes I took and the people I met changed my mind and I wanted very much to teach. I graduated with honors and taught third grade in a diversified urban setting for nine years.

You, Lord Jesus, are the Master Teacher with the highest of standards.
Forgive me for my wrongs while teaching so many vulnerable children.
And be with me as I continue to both teach and be taught.

Through Hugo's encouragement and your answers to my many prayers,
I finally finished my book about what distinguishes the best teachers.
It was a huge, lengthy job but you helped me to persevere with it.

During the second half of my life I've taken a wide varity of classes.
I've studied speed reading, bookkeeping, computer, harmonica...
And I've taught, lectured, organized dramatic presentations, etc.

What About You?

1. What does the word *teach* mean in your life?

2. What were Jesus' main teachings? Which speak(s) the loudest to you at this point in time?

3. What expertise, skill, or experience do you have that you could teach to others?

Imagine

March 6, 2010

Where would we be today if the people of the past hadn't used their imaginations? Long before we drove around in automobiles, flew from place to place, and stepped foot on the moon *someone* (actually many people) had to first imagine it. Just think about all the things we use each day that are truly incredible... electricity, computers, pain-killers, telephones (and the list goes on an on). And the most amazing of all is life itself—our bodies, our brains, and our natural world teeming with intricacies we've only begun to discover. Obviously, we're a "chip off the old block." We're made in God's image, and have inherited a portion of his great imagination!

The winter Olympics in Canada just ended and the feats of the participants were astounding. A large part of their success surely lay in the use of their God-given imaginations. Every single medal winner had no doubt imagined receiving that medal countless times before it became reality. The late Viktor Frankl, a renowned psychologist, survived a Nazi concentration camp while so many others perished. He imagined himself again and again surviving the death camp and standing in front of a huge crowd, telling them about his experience there. His book, "Man's Search for Meaning," now carries his story to future generations.

"If we can imagine it, we can realize it" should be a saying. In fact, what we imagine is often dwarfed by what actually happens. A good example is Walt Disney. Inspired by a pet mouse he once had, he imagined it coming to life as a cartoon character. What he never imagined was how much goodness Mickey would bring to a world in need wholesome laughter.

*John Lennon's song "Imagine" tells of a world without greed or hunger,
where sharing is the norm and people sincerely care for each other.
He died a violent death but his song and vision live on.*

*Martin Luther King had a dream that all people would be treated equally,
judged not by the color of their skin but the content of their character.
He also died violently, but his dream continues to inspire and guide.*

*Paul told how God's work in us far exceeds imaginations (Eph. 3:20).
Imagine Paul's amazement at all he accomplished for the Lord!
He died violently, too. But his work and words still affect us.*

What About You?

1. What have *you* imagined that has actualized in some form? How did the actual compare to the imagined?

2. What are you imagining right now that you'd love to see realized?

3. Which belief about God most powerfully sparks your imagination? How can you act on it?

Ask

March 8, 2010

It was an ideal day (sunny, blue sky, in the 50's) great for walking the dog and doing what our word-of-the-day tells us to do. So, I walked and asked the Lord for:

* qualities I sorely need: wisdom, discernment, humility, compassion, and understanding.
* blessings on friends and loved ones, help with projects, guidance in decision-making, etc.

Jesus said:

> If you have faith when you pray, you will be given whatever you ask for. (Matt. 21:22)
> Ask, and it will be given to you. (Matt. 7:7 and Luke 11:9)
> Ask in my name, then it will be given to you, so you'll be completely happy. (John 16:24)

As a child I didn't ask for too much—we didn't have all the tempting "stuff" we have today. But when I *really* wanted something my parents sacrificed to get it for me: a bicycle, a piano, a cat... Mercifully they ignored ridiculous or inappropriate requests, like my desire to have a horse or go hunting (Thank heaven!) God responds to our requests in a similar way. We don't always get what we want, but we know he loves us and will help us deal with unanswered prayer.

An unknown veteran of the Civil War wrote this in the 1900s:

> I asked for strength that I might achieve; I was made weak that I might humbly learn to obey.
> I asked for health to do greater things; I was given infirmity that I might do better things.
> I asked for riches that I might be happy; I was given poverty that I might be wise.
> I asked for power to get the praise of men; I was given weakness to feel the need of God.
> I asked for all things that I might enjoy life; I was given life that I might enjoy all things.
> I got nothing that I asked for, but everything that I had hoped for.
> I am, among all men, most richly blessed.

*Asking the right question makes all the difference. JFK told us to
ask "What can I do for our country?" instead of asking the opposite.
Let's ask the Lord what we can do for him and what he can do <u>with</u> us.*

*When I ask God's help I do things a lot better.
I have to ask more often—and ask others to help me, too.
And I must be ready to respond when others ask my help.*

*Thanks, Lord, for being the greatest advisor and consultant of all.
I know I can run anything by you and you will respond somehow.
What more could anyone ask? I am completely happy and richly blessed.*

What About You?

1. Paul asked God repeatedly to remove the "thorn in his flesh" but God
    refused, saying: *My grace is sufficient for you, for power is perfected in
    weakness.* Check out Paul's reaction in 2 Corinthians 12:9-10. When
    has God not granted your request, and how did you handle it?

2. What examples do you have of *answered* prayer, yours or another's?

3. What should you be asking God for right this minute? What is stopping
    you?

Compare

March 15, 2010

Compare is a perfect word for a day when we have no electricity. I'm actually writing this three days later, based on notes I took as this challenging day unfolded. But what an object lesson it provides, similar to the prophets who were told to do symbolic things, like Hosea marrying a harlot, Jeremiah buying land but not getting married, Isaiah walking around Jerusalem naked and barefoot, and Ezekiel shaving his beard in a special way. Even Jesus' clearing of the temple can be seen as a prophetic act.

The lesson I embody from three days without electricity (after a huge nor'easter on top of a heavy-snow blizzard) is this: *When we compare our situation to others, we see how easy we have it.* Even though we lost half of our almost-flowering magnolia tree and a big 50-foot spruce tree in the two storms, we had no basement flooding as many did, because their pumps didn't work. We lost the use of our refrigerator and freezer but we were able to cook on our gas burners. Friends even brought over dry ice and a battery-powered lamp to ease our inconveniences.

Recent earthquakes in Haiti and Chile make all of our inconveniences pale when compared to their tragedies. It makes me realize that I am living a very luxurious life, often wasting time, effort, and money on things that don't have any lasting value. It's perhaps time to compare the way I'm now living to how I should and could be living in light of eternity. Am I too busy building up treasures on earth to give much thought or action to building up treasures in heaven?

Help us, Lord, to compare our treasures on earth to our heavenly ones.
Help us to see ways we can better balance these treasures.
Help us to use all we are and have for your glorious purposes.

I'm thankful indeed to see the progress my broken wrist has made.
A former boyfriend just died. I thought about my life with and
without his influence and the goodness he brought to it.

The more I compare, the better I see my many blessings. Thank you!
Let me be generous in using and sharing them, and
let me not compare myself to others, but to the growth I'm making.

What About You?

1. How do your treasures on earth compare to your treasures in heaven?

2. What comparisons are you presently making? Are they taking you in God's direction?

3. What do you see when you compare your life today to your life years ago? And your life today to the life you'd like to live? What conclusions result?

Laugh

March 16, 2010

Now here's a happy word to think about today. It's been proven that laughter is great holistic medicine. Norman Cousins got several additional years of life by laughing himself healthier. He watched funny movies, like Laurel and Hardy, to trigger the release of the happiness hormone, serotonin—the one that makes us feel better. And his body responded accordingly.

I'm generally a happy person, but I admit that I could be a tad more cheerful when salespeople call on the telephone (during dinner, of course). I sometimes answer a most welcome call with a bit of an attitude, suspecting it to be pesky one—then I'm reminded that it's better to be kind at all times so I don't miss the angels God might be sending my way. (See Hebrew 13:2)

It's such fun to have a really hearty laugh, isn't it? I got some great laughs reading *Before the Dog can Eat Your Homework, First You Have to Do It*, a book by John O'Hurley, who is J. Peterman on the "Seinfeld" TV show. And just today I borrowed a book from our health club reading room because I was "in stitches" just reading the first couple of pages. The Book? Erma Bombeck's "Family—the Ties that Bind...and Gag!"

I've been blessed by a dad who had a clever wit and now a husband (and pets) that keep me laughing. Our neighbor hit it on the head recently when she talked about the three things that make for a good marriage: love, respect, and a sense of humor!

Laughter is fun—and contagious. It gets even better when it's shared.
One of the lessons in our book "Bark Up the Right Tree" is:
Happiness Shared is Happiness Multiplied—a motto for my emails.

Laughter is healthy, because it influences our feel-good hormones.
Proverbs (17:22) tells us that a joyful heart is good medicine.
A wholesome laugh that lifts our spirits is especially exhilarating.

Laughter is a gauge: a person's character is revealed by what s/he laughs at.
Foolish laughter is stupid (Ec 7:6), and derisive laughter is hurtful.
But a God with a sense of humor makes life a joyous adventure.

What About You?

1. When have you or others said, "God must have a sense of humor!"?

2. What makes *you* laugh? When was your last uncontrollable belly laugh?

3. When has a laugh hurt you or someone else? What lessons did or can you learn from such occasions?

Edify

March 17, 2010

The definition of *edify* is "to improve or uplift morally." It's not a word we often use, but St. Paul does—when he instructs the new Christians to edify each other as they follow after the things that make for peace. He tells the Roman believers to please others, help them, and build them up...edification, for sure!

I'm now thinking of the word in terms of my own thoughts, words, and deeds. Do they spread goodness? Are they helpful? Do they glorify God? (Would they make my mother proud of me?) Everything starts with our thoughts. That's why Paul says to think about things that are excellent and worthy of praise (Phil 4:8). And God promises that he will keep us in perfect peace if our minds are stayed on him (Is 26:3) because it edifies us, and then we, in turn, can edify others.

As we spend our time and money, and use our God-given talents, it's good to keep this word in mind. By asking "Is this edifying?" before we speak or act we can filter out temptations and distractions that divert us from our high ideals and God-pleasing pursuits. It's frightening to see the caliber of our reading and viewing fare nowadays—and its effect on our society. Even when the stories are good they generally contain speech and scenes that a generation ago would not have been permitted. I'm very concerned for our children, who are being surrounded with so many "less than edifying" ideas, materials, and examples. "Adult entertainment" should be something youngsters aspire to because of its high-minded and noble content.

Help me, Lord, to bring to the world words and deeds that edify.
I'll think before I speak or act, and use my time in edifying ways.
I'll reap the strength and satisfaction of choosing the high road.

It's such fun to help others because it's edifying to us as well as to them.
I'll strive to teach people to "fish" rather than giving them a fish.
It's better to empower and encourage than do too much for someone.

Help me, Lord, to model what it means to listen well and empathize.
Help me to point people in your direction, then step back and
let go rather than holding on too tightly or being too controlling.

What About You?

1. What do you find edifying for you? How do you edify others?

2. What would you make more edifying, if you could? What step(s) can you take in that direction?

3. They say, "No good deed goes unpunished." When have your or others' good intentions fallen short of their goals? What might have changed the outcome(s)?

Change

March 20, 2010

One of the things we can definitely rely on in life is change. Want it or not, we're saddled with it--a good reminder that everything on earth is temporary, including us. The Bible is full of change. Boy, did Adam and Eve's situation ever change when they disobeyed God! And Jesus was (and still is) a master of change, because He changes people's lives dramatically. St. Paul talks about the change in those who are courageous enough to believe in Jesus even though they have never seen him. In 2 Co 5:17 he says: *Anyone who belongs to Christ is a new person. The past is forgotten, and everything is new.* That's us, right?

This has been a big year of change for me. A high school classmate (Barbara) and I were brought together by the "Classmates" website, and together we created a dates-to-remember book called "Rescued Dogs on the Go!" Barbara did the photography and I did the writing. We now sell our book, along with Jessie's "Bark Up the Right Tree" book, to support animal rescue groups and their activities. I've also learned a great deal in the past twelve months and have made some wonderful friends through our two big fundraisers, *Dogfest* and *Pets & Heroes*. And my "agnostic" hubby, Hugo, is very much a part of these good things—truly an answer to prayer.

Then there's our little granddaughter Jessica whose first year on earth was nothing short of astounding, and our new pastor, Chuck Holm, bringing good changes to our church. Other recent but not-so-enjoyable changes were my first broken bone, losing a good friend to cancer, and almost losing my brother to a heart attack. Thankfully, a constant Friend was with me.

How comforting it is to know that you are changeless, Lord, and that
the eternal life you promise comes with new, more favorable rules.
It's especially hard for us to let go of loved ones here on earth.

Change me, Lord, so I'll be the person you want me to be.
Let me know what it is that needs changing so I can help out on this end.
Increase my equanimity and trust so that changes won't overpower me.

What can I change in addition to myself, Lord?
Please show me what needs changing and how I can best help.
Search me, try me, and lead me in the way everlasting (per Ps 139).

What About You?

1. What type of changes do you find most difficult? Most delightful? Most comforting?

2. What has changed your life for the better? How has God helped you through changes that challenge or devastate?

3. What Biblical (and other) examples come to *your* mind as you ponder the verb *change*?

Bloom

March 21, 2010

What better word could I ask for on this first day of spring? I started the day with a lovely pre-breakfast walk with my dog, Jessie—waiting to see what word would call my name. It wasn't until I sat down to breakfast and Joel Osteen's TV sermon that the word made itself known. Joel talked about blooming where we're planted, making the most out of where we are today and not letting anything steal our joy. *Bloom* was it, our word for today!

Then off to church I went, where I didn't have to think twice about signing on for some memorial flowers to grace the Easter alter. I ordered three pots of tulips, one in memory of all the loved ones who have left me a legacy of goodness and love, one in honor of a special friend and her family, and one in honor of Jessica Ruth, our baby granddaughter. After the Easter service I'll give my friend hers and keep the other two for our house.

Now some serious thought is in order as I consider whether or not I qualify as one who blooms where s/he is planted. I think I'm pretty good at that. I recall working long hours at our international marketing firm—sometimes even overnights that would stretch into the next workday (people probably wondered why I was wearing the same outfit two days in a row). Thankfully, that meant we needed more help and additional people were gradually hired. Even though I preferred to be out doing more for the Lord and others, I put my heart into learning all I could about "keeping books" and managing a company or organization. And sure enough, several years later I started our charitable foundation and could finally use those skills and experiences for God's good purposes.

Lilies-of-the-valley grace our garden walk; as do purple buds of myrtle.
Spring is here! It's about time for plants to bloom—and me, too!
I plan to give to and take from each day as much as I possibly can.

Blooming means taking a risk; some blustery weather may still be ahead.
It means absorbing the nurturing power that only God can provide,
drinking in the rain, basking in the sun, and bending with the wind.

Blooming means delighting in our own uniqueness without envying others.
It means adding color, fragrance, and beauty to a world in need of it,
coming forth when called, and faithfully yielding when time is up.

What About You?

1. When have *you* bloomed where you were planted? How did it work out?

2. Joel Osteen talked about Joseph in Genesis and our pastor talked about Esther's story in the Book of Esther. Both are good examples of people who bloomed where they were planted. Who do you know (or know of) who is another good example?

3. How and why is blooming where we're planted both a gift *from* God and a gift *to* God?

Participate

March 22, 2010

It's always a balancing act deciding what to say yes to and what to forego. My life has gotten so busy that I've pretty much taken my hubby's advice and try to participate just in those worthwhile things that only I can do and/or that wouldn't get done unless I do them. Definitely not committee work, because it's not my forte...plus it generally gets done very well without me.

So I've been busy this past decade creating and leading/co-facilitating unique things like the 6-session Happiness Workshop, the Stories-Stories (storytelling) course, and a wide variety of Bible Studies with titles like *Bible Read-Thru, Finding Answers through Biblical Questions, Lessons to Live By, and Scripture a Week to Make Us Strong.* In coordination with these I've written many newsletters—and presently I do a Woof-a-Week newsletter/commentary using the voice of my dog Jessie. I feel as if God will keep the creativity flowing as long as I keep writing, so I never want to stop. These Word-a-Day writings are another example of something I've said yes to because it's something that is unique to me and takes me in God's direction.

Even though I already have a lot on my "plate" at the moment, I just couldn't resist saying yes to being a narrator for our Easter Cantata next Sunday—it's just one practice so it isn't a big commitment. I also think I'll sign up for one of our new pastor's Bible classes this spring. The topic is "change," which just happens to be a recent word of the day—for March 20th, to be exact. I look forward to participating in both of these opportunities for spiritual growth.

Help me, Lord, in choosing how to spend my limited time and energy.
Jesus said the harvest is plentiful, but the workers are few (Mt 7:37).
May I always be your worker, one who needn't be ashamed (2 Ti 2:15).

As a child I wanted to be in Girl Scouts and Cherub Choir, but couldn't.
So I kept pestering to play a musical instrument until I could!
Other times, teachers saw my shyness and pushed me to participate.

I'm not so shy now because I focus on things far bigger than myself.
There's no time for shyness with so many good things to be done.
Like Isaiah, I want to say: Here I am, Lord--send me!

What About You?

1. What have you wanted to participate in sometime in your past, but never did? Is there anything you can do about it now?

2. What type of opportunities do you generally say yes to? Which do you generally forego?

3. What are you passionate about? Are there any unique opportunities you yourself can create to share your passion(s) with others?

Stop

March 23, 2010

An interesting word... especially because I seem to have a real problem stopping certain things—like eating snack food. Not only do I have an irresistible attraction to things like M&M's, chips, ice cream, Panda Puffs, and Girl Scout Cookies, but once I start eating them I keep going. I can eat a large bag of M&M's or a (now downsized) half-gallon of ice cream in a day or two, and the entire box of puffs or cookies in one sitting!

I also battle with other obsessions, like earlier this week when I was looking for plane tickets for my daughter and family to visit us the first two weeks in May. I searched both new and favorite websites, some more than once. I kept at it for a good part of my working day, not wanting to give up until it was settled. Meanwhile I called Elisa and/or Danny several times until we thought it was settled. Then I just *had* to try one more possibility with a couple of advantages over the tickets we'd ordered. I ended up ordering two sets of tickets, calling family again, having them label me "possessed," and then canceling the second set of tickets anyway.

Then there are bigger things that should be stopped—things I have less control over, but can certainly do something about. For example, blatant abuses of children, women, and animals throughout the world—and right in our own neighborhood. Our non-profit (Open Doors, an Amazing Grace Foundation) is an advocate for both children and animals in need. We do this by producing books, having fundraisers, and supporting those doing the front line work. It's an honor to support those who act so selflessly on their desire to stop as much suffering as they can.

It was good for me to stop once in awhile today and check things out.
Too bad I didn't stop when I started eating that box of Panda Puffs!
Help me, Lord, to stop unhealthy habits so I can better serve you.

Help me to see more clearly what needs to be stopped, such as
my doing lesser tasks in lieu the important ones, and
my frittering away time/money that can be put to better uses.

Help me to shout "Stop!" when something needs correcting—in myself, in
society, in others (coupled with diplomacy and compassion, of course).
May I never stop growing, loving, dreaming, and working for you, Lord.

What About You?

1.   What do you see in yourself, the world, etc. that needs to be stopped?
     What can you *do* about it?

2.   What should you strive to *never* stop?

3.   How can we stop sensible things (like snacking and helping family)
     from turning into negative, obsessive things?

Love

March 25, 2010

My only surprise with this word is that it didn't pop up sooner. John says that God *is* love (I Jo 4:16) and listens to those who love and obey him. Peter (I:4:8) says that we should love each other because love covers a multitude of sins. Paul ends his famous Love Chapter (1 Corinthians 13) by saying that of these three great things—faith, hope, and love—the greatest is love. And Jesus says we must love the Lord with all our heart, soul, mind, and strength; and we must also love others as much as we love ourselves.

People who claim to be religious, but hurt others, are far from God, *not* near him. My husband, Hugo, calls himself an agnostic but he recognizes Christian love. If we go to a store and the clerk is especially cheerful and helpful, he'll whisper to me "Here's another born-again Christian!" And he enjoys pastor Joel Osteen on TV because his message is always practical and loving.

One of my favorite songs is "They'll Know We are Christians by our Love." And one line, *We'll guard each one's dignity and save each one's pride*, has always had special meaning for me because that's where I have a tendency to fall short. I've hurt people (and myself), and continue to do so, by careless words. I say too much, too soon, too often, and at the wrong times. I know I can draw much closer to God by being more discreet with my words. I need to weigh my words carefully before uttering them. It's hard to imagine that I was once so shy my elementary speech teacher later confessed to me that she worried I wouldn't be able to function in adult society. Now I must be careful not to let my words get out of control!

Love is listening better, talking less, doing more good things, forgetting self in service of others, seeing things from others' perspectives, showing kindness, and forgiving when tempted to do otherwise.

Love is being punctual and reliable, shedding light on an injustice, doing thoughtful and practical things that mean a lot to others, encouraging people, enjoying their successes instead of being jealous.

Love is caring for our pets, helping a neighbor (or stranger), writing that note, not being concerned about getting the credit or the accolades, and putting God first and foremost in our lives.

What About You?

1. Who is the most loving person you know, or know of? Why do you choose him or her?

2. How is love given and received in *your* everyday life?

3. What can we do to increase the love in our lives, and in the world?

Shine

March 30, 2010

We've had lots of rain and clouds this past week, but hallelujah! The sun has finally started to shine again—what a difference, and what a joy! I guess God wants to remind us that we can spread sunshine, too, and brighten up the world around us. In Matthew 5:16 Jesus says, *Make your light shine, so that others will see the good you do and will praise your Father in heaven.*

Coincidentally, I've been noticing my need to be more consistently kind and cheerful, even when talking with irksome people by telephone, or requesting a refund based on some sort of complaint. There's no reason I can't remain even-tempered and considerate in all instances. I can "speak the truth in love." In fact, I'm probably more likely to get what I want, and bring out the best in others, by polishing up my shine a bit too (maybe even *quite a bit!*)

Wouldn't it be marvelous if people could look at me and think of God? And how honored I'd be to have my face reflect God's glory… or to be so lovingly transparent that people would look right through me to God. Well, that isn't going to happen unless I use my gifts to shine and, at the same time, be humble enough to forget self, love others, and credit God.

My shine has to come from God-shine. One of my favorite Scriptures is Numbers 6:24-26: *The LORD bless you and keep you: The LORD make his face to shine upon you, and be gracious to you: The LORD lift up his countenance upon you, and give you peace.* This lovely blessing has been used for centuries and has inspired countless people, including me!

Help me, Lord, to seek/find your Light so it shines on and through me.
Quiet meditation to Gregorian chants helped me draw closer to you.
Sometimes I still see that comforting brightness when I close my eyes.

I've gotten away from that discipline—and the brightness has dimmed.
Please rekindle that flame, dear Lord, by sending your God-shine,
a never-fading brightness that comes from deep within.

It can shine on loved ones, acquaintances, and folks I may never meet.
I'll radiate your love, forgiveness, wisdom, strength…
With your help it can be so. I'm sure of it!

What About You?

1.   What are some ways in which we can all let our lights shine?

2.   Who do you know who radiates God love? How does he/she do it?

3.   What can *you* do to polish up *your* shine?

Learn

March 31, 2010

I always enjoyed learning things that interested me. I pretended to write (with squiggly lines) long before I really knew how--and I loved it when my brother helped me to learn U.S. Geography and all of the state capitals at a very young age. As a young adult, I enjoyed trying things like cutting hair, tap-dancing, strumming the guitar, becoming intimately familiar with the Bible...

I love the fact that learning is ongoing. As seniors Hugo and I are still very much in the learning mode. We have yet to go into a library without finding a "must read" book or two or three... and we're always up for another adventure in learning (a seminar, a course, or perhaps an Elderhostel trip). My thirst for knowledge and God is strong and I plan to never stop feeling it and seeking to quench it. I just signed up to take a fascinating seven-week course being offered by our new pastor; it's called "A Faith for All Seasons" and focuses on dealing with change.

The Bible mentions learning to fear God, learning God's statutes and commandments, and learning righteousness. Matthew 11:29 records Jesus saying: *Learn of me, for I am meek and lowly and your souls will find rest.* He couples it with *Take my yoke upon you,* which puts some legs to our learning. What good is learning unless we put it to good use? When I learned the entire Book of Mark by heart I felt a call to lead a Bible study that involved my telling it and inviting others to participate by learning and telling the stories, too. As a special Mother's Day "sermon" seven of us told some of Mark's stories verbatim--dressed appropriately as a reminder that the stories of Jesus were first told orally.

78

We can learn from every situation and person we encounter in life...
lessons that enrich, inspire, and encourage us.
Let's pass them on to as many others as we possibly can.

Reading is a gift that unlocks mysteries, imparts knowledge, and expands
both mind and soul with new ideas and experiences.
I recently read a story I'd like to share with you:

A woman had a valuable stone. A man admired it, and she gave it to him!
He left, thrilled with his good luck. But he soon gave it back, saying:
"What I really want is what enabled you to give me that stone!"

What About You?

1.   What do you think enabled the woman to give the stone away? Why is it more valuable than the stone?

2.   What lessons have *you* learned in life that you would like to pass on to others?

3.   Is there something you're thirsting to learn or do? If so, why not do it-- or at least get a taste of it?

Exercise

April 1, 2010

Here's something we can probably all use more of—*exercise*, for our bodies and/or our brains. My junior high school Latin teacher, Mr. Cotter, would periodically have a class-participation exercise he called "mental gymnastics" (something we all feared.) He would pose a question to us in perfect Latin and expect us to answer it in like manner. I was so frightened of his class I studied like crazy—and ended up tutoring Latin later that year. It was my first paid job.

In 1967 I married a man who has encouraged and joined me over the years in taking long walks and working out at health spas. Hugo is turning 81 next month and is in excellent health. The only thing he has to watch is the PSI level on his prostate gland. I'm doing well with my health, too, and I'm sure the regular walking, work-outs, and swimming have been instrumental in keeping my attitude up and my weight down.

So why would God ask me to contemplate this word if I'm already exercising my body—and my brain, too? Memorizing so much of the Bible during the past decade has kept my mind limber, as has my reading and constant learning. I'm not a puzzle-loving person like my mom was with her many crossword challenges. But I do use my brain to create projects, some of which I actually carry through on. And I'm an avid writer as you may have noticed. I'm ready to write the sequel to our *Bark up the Right Tree* book; I just need the time to do it--maybe after the Book Launch for the first book, and the big Dogfest Fun'raiser during the summer. Perhaps I should think more deeply about the spiritual aspect of this word...

I need the kind of exercise that will bring me closer to you, Lord:
I must exercise my faith by learning, praying, and doing more.
I must also exercise good judgment and caution in speech and actions.

By exercising my patience, so I'll be a better waiter and listener.
With more sound thinking and common sense I'll avoid hurting others,
and my time and energy will be well spent on your behalf.

Help me to be more disciplined and thoughtful of others, dear Lord.
Stretch my ambitions, my trust in you, my ability to communicate…
and my understanding of your will for the remainder of my life.

What About You?

1. How have you been exercising well, and not so well?

2. What should you ask God to help you with (including things you've been avoiding)?

3. How can you exercise your prerogative (exclusive right or privilege) as a US citizen? A world citizen? A child of God?

Praise

April 4, 2010

Praise the Lord! It's Easter Sunday, my favorite day of the year. Because of the Jesus' resurrection we were able to visit the cemetery today and I could confidently tell deceased loved ones that we look forward to seeing them again.

Praise the Lord for his church here on earth! Even Hugo, my "agnostic" husband accompanied me today to help with the tulips I'd ordered in memory of loved ones and in honor of friends and our new granddaughter, Jessica Ruth. And in the process we heard uplifting music—trumpet and all, and a sermon that focused on what Easter is all about: pardon for the past, power for the present, and promise for the future.

Praise the Lord for those precious people whose paths cross ours as we journey through life! At church I spoke with a young man who sang in my children's choir a generation ago. He now has a lovely wife and two beautiful children. Later in the day we used our computer to meet some newcomers to our family—our daughter's new relatives in Florida. Praise God for so many amazing inventions, like Skype, which enabled us to both see and talk to these wonderful people.

Praise the Lord for his amazing creation! We walked in the sunshine and enjoyed the blossoming bushes. We took Jessie the dog with us; she seemed to have more energy than ever—perhaps she, too, is full of praise for things she can't verbalize. As we walked, we met friends we hadn't seen in awhile and exchanged pleasantries with folks we didn't know.

Praise for our spiritual forebears, who spread the Good News,
for Christian programs, books and music to uplift us and glorify God,
for those we know personally who truly live their faith.

I stayed up late tonight to see a great movie on the Gospel Music Channel.
The film was called "Peter and Paul" with Anthony Hopkins as Paul.
Others were James, John, Barnabus, Timothy, Mark, Luke, and Silas.

This movie made me aware of the praiseworthy efforts of so many in
setting up the first churches, ironing out the controversies, and
doing God's will amid so many challenges and difficulties.

What About You?

1. What challenges and difficulties face the church today? What praiseworthy efforts, individuals, and groups come to the fore?

2. *Praise the Lord, for he is good. His mercy endures forever.* What are some wonderful Psalms of praise that can inspire and strengthen us?

3. What fills you with praise today? How does praise benefit the one doing the praising?

Lead

April 9, 2010

We all have leadership potential built into us by a loving Creator. We just fail to recognize and use it. We're born free of self-consciousness, inferiority complexes, and all those learned stumbling blocks. I recall when my sister and I were in the single-digit ages we attended a show with our aunt and uncle. There were banjo players, and a magician who called my sister and me up for a special trick or two. He was surprised that my sister knew there were 52 cards in a deck (*I* wouldn't have known). He brought *me* into the action by placing a rubber snake on my shoulder and said he'd bring it to life by saying some magic words. He elongated it as much as possible so the audience could enjoy my panicked face. Fortunately the trick didn't work.

A few years later, however, that trick (and other memorable experiences) took their toll on my personality: I'd no longer run enthusiastically up onto a stage, and when a classmate brought a snake to school for show and tell, I would run to the back of room to avoid it. I was terribly shy—and deathly afraid of animal heads because my brother said they'd come off the wall and eat me. To this day I hate snakes and hesitate whenever I enter a new place--for fear of heads.

The sum of my leadership roles early in life consisted of being a safety patrol in fifth grade, which meant wearing a white shoulder belt--and rising to lieutenant in sixth grade, when I got to strap a metal badge onto my arm. As a pre-teen I was nominated and voted in as secretary to the JIF (Junior Intermediate Fellowship) at our church—and did a decent job (but nothing to brag about, since I seem to recall not even attending all the meetings.)

Thankfully, God works with us when we're open to his leading. Through good times and bad we stuck together; gradually I gained confidence. I went to college, sang in the church choir, and drew closer to him.

I went from babysitter to playground leader, teacher, wife, and mother. Then the baton was in my hand as I directed children's choirs and became an amateur playwright, writer, mentor, and speaker.

I'll do whatever you ask, Lord. Thanks for bringing me to this hour. Please send others to love and bless those I've hurt, and let me touch those others have hurt and lead them to you!

What About You?

1. In John 1:45-51 we find the disciple Philip leading his friend, Nathanael (who also became a disciple) to Jesus. Who have you influenced--either purposely or without having realized it until you were made aware of it?

2. How have your leadership skills improved over the years?

3. Good leaders make good followers and vice versa. How are you ready and/or not so ready to follow the Lord into new and challenging positions of leadership?

Imitate

This is a good word for me because I've been quite an imitator my entire life. Growing up, I imitated my sister Janet (just 22 months my elder) a lot! Whatever she wanted (a Hopalong Cassidy outfit, a new bicycle, etc.) I did, too. We played on the same playground baseball team, had the same friends, were baptized and confirmed together, double-dated once in awhile, and eventually became God-parent to each other's daughters. She was generally a great role model--it was because of her that I learned the Books of the Bible, the Ten Commandments, the Beatitudes, and the 23rd Psalm. She wanted to earn the reward--so I did, too. But the greatest reward was experiencing early on how wonderful it is to know and love God's Word.

Unfortunately, I have sometimes imitated things that haven't been so good. I started to curse, imitating people on the playground—until my older brother heard me and hit me on the head with a rolled-up newspaper, making me promise never to use those words again. Another time I joined a "lynch mob" and tormented a girl from our church by singing "We hate you 24 hours a day..." and "You weigh sixteen tons..." (take-offs on popular songs). Amazingly, she forgave us and today we're faith-filled friends. And now I try to imitate *her*!

On my first day as a new teacher I did many good things...and one terrible thing. I ripped up a child's paper and scolded him in front of the class—something I'd seen my supervising teacher do when I was student teaching. The paper wasn't even that bad; I was just out to show who's boss the way she did. To this day the thought of it humiliates me (and the child, too, I'm sure).

Fortunately I had 179 more school days to make amends to the student.
I hope and pray that no one will imitate any of my horrible actions!
I've learned that when I hurt others I hurt you, Lord—and myself, too.

I regret not having been more compassionate, unselfish, and genuine.
Thanks to your and others' love, I now go forward stronger and better
while striving to imitate Jesus and those who act most like him.

I took notes as I read Thomas a'Kempis' classic, "Imitation of Christ."
Its wisdom inspired me to do an original writing of my own called
"Following Jesus Today and Every Day: Ways to Walk in His Footsteps."

What About You?

1. Who have *you* imitated, and who imitates you?

2. When have you imitated the wrong thing? Which of your imitations are you most proud of and thankful for?

3. Paul said to the Ephesians 5:1: *Be imitators of God as dearly loved children.* How can we best follow this command?

Fear

The word *fear* is mentioned 385 times in the King James version of the Bible. So it's not surprising that it's one of the 366 words we'll be focusing on this year. It's not generally a feel-good word, but when used to mean awe and reverence (as in *The fear of the Lord is the beginning of wisdom*, in Psalms, and *It shall be well with them that fear God*, in Ecclesiastes) it lifts us and reminds us of our total dependence on God.

There is also some "fear meaning fright" in our relation to God, because God has complete control over us and everything else. How can we not be afraid of *that*? Matthew tells us that when Jesus sent his disciples out for a "test run," he told them not to fear people who kill the body—but to fear God, who can destroy *both* body and soul in hell. There's a line in John Newton's song, "Amazing Grace," that reminds us that God's greatness both invokes and calms our fears: *'Twas grace that taught my heart to fear; and grace my fear relieved.*

God does what God wants for God's own reasons. None of us has any say in that. But amazingly, as referred to in the song, the more we respect, honor, and reverence the Lord the more God shows his mercy and assures us that we're on the winning side! And in some miraculous way, God knows us intimately and answers our prayers—and makes promises that enable us to say (as in the Gaither song): *Because Christ lives I can face tomorrow; because he lives all fear is gone...*

Healthy fear gets us to obey rules, drive carefully, make wise choices…
but extreme or irrational fear can cripple us and take over our lives.
Prayer and faith are powerful weapons against these unhealthy fears.

The command to "Fear not" appears 62 times in the King James Bible,
from God telling Abram in Genesis: "Fear not. I'm your shield and reward,"
to Jesus saying in Revelation: "Fear not. I am the first and the last."

F.D. R. said, "We've nothing to fear but fear itself." So, when fears comes
my way I'll think of our merciful, omnipotent God and ask for his help.
Thanks, dear Lord, for handling my fears both with and for me!"

What About You?

1. How has fear been a part of *your* life?

2. What fears are you contending with today?

3. How can we use our spiritual armor (See Ephesians 6:10-17) and the knowledge of God's great merciful love to ward off and handle our fears?

Agree

April 17, 2010

There's power in agreement. Jesus tells us to unite in prayer, promising that where two or three are gathered he will surely be there. And in Matthew 18:19 he makes this amazing statement: *I promise that when any two of you on earth agree about something you are praying for, my Father in heaven will do it for you.*

Jesus also tells us to be peacemakers and agree even with our adversaries, for practical as well as spiritual reasons (See Mt 5:25). And he tells us not to even approach God if we remember that someone is angry with us. We're instructed in Mt 5:23-23 to go and make peace with that person *before* we turn our attention to God.

When we find common ground (even if it means "agreeing to amicably disagree" as Hugo and I sometimes do) we can enrich each other's lives without seeing eye-to-eye on everything. Disagreements do not have to mean arguing; they can foster growth. It's been said that if two people agree on everything, one of them is unnecessary!

Looking back, I see times when I've lost entire relationships (often with lingering bad feelings) because I was unwilling or afraid to approach people to confess or even discuss the sensitive matters. I have also been too easily swayed to agree, or have remained silent, when I should have stood up and/or spoken up to express my true opinion. For these faults I ask forgiveness and pray for wisdom, discernment, and courage to act differently going forward.

90

When we don't agree on Bible-related things, I think you understand, Lord.
Why argue about the trees (details) and miss the forest (the big picture)?
We are the clay and you are the potter; mold us and use us for good.

Paul said: "Get along... Don't take sides. Always try to agree..." (I Co 1:10)
Peter said: "Agree and have concern and love for each other." (I Pe 3:8)
Help us do this, Lord, even when agreement seems almost impossible.

Let's watch what we agree to and how we sway others with words/actions.
May we strive to draw closer to God and bring others closer, too,
so we can be united as one in the New Agreement offered by our Savior.

What About You?

1. When have you failed to agree when you should have, and vice versa? And when has your agreement, disagreement , or silence been exactly the right thing to do?

2. Paul used occasions of disagreement as opportunities to tell people about God and Jesus (See Acts 17). How can we do the same in our contemporary environment?

3. What doubts and disagreements do you harbor in regard to the Bible? How can these bring you closer to God?

Delve

April 18, 2010

We certainly don't want to delve into other people's business, do we? Unfortunately it's human nature to do so, judging from the variety of gossipy newspapers and TV shows. That type of delving is something I must lessen and avoid. I must get into the habit of squelching the type of curiosity that leads me into juicy stories about others (even if they're celebrities and I'd be just one of millions drinking it all in).

What I do need to do more and better is looking more deeply into people's eyes and hearts. I must consider the histories, reasons, motives, and circumstances of people and situations. I tend to take things at surface value. This has resulted in my being duped into trusting people I never should have, and being nasty with people when kindness and understanding would have been much more effective and helpful.

What we all need to delve more deeply into is God's Word. The rewards are boundless. I grew up with a fearsome awe (and awesome fear) of the Bible, particularly the King James Version. I initially thought it was handed to us by God himself, much the way Hollywood portrayed God giving Moses the Ten Commandments. Even when I realized that wasn't the case, I regarded the Bible as far above me, powerful and holy—and hard to understand. The parts I knew were beautiful (no translation can match their eloquence), but I shied away from the rest of it even though I thirsted for more. I recall, in my early thirties, admiring our pastor for his deep knowledge of the Scriptures, and thinking: "If only I could approach the Bible, be comfortable with it, and mine its riches."

*As my desire to know the Bible grew stronger I grew more knowledgeable.
I went to Bible studies and read through a modern version--with
guides like Bible Pathway and The Daily Walk. It was great!*

*The amazing thing about the Bible is that it has many layers, and each
time I delve into it I find something new speaking to my heart.
I'm finally comfortable with it, and love to mine its riches!*

*Encouraging others' interest in the Bible led me to delve even deeper.
I read, attended courses, asked questions, and used reference aids like
Barclay Commentary, Revell Bible Dictionary and SearchGodsWord.Org.*

What About You?

1. What has captivated you *so* much that you have delved deeply into mastering it?

2. Is there something you would like to delve more deeply into, but haven't done so thus far? How might you ease into it as I did with my interest in the Bible?

3. What are some ways in which you can look more deeply into the "eyes" of the God who loves you so?

Handle

April 20, 2010

I think (hope) I can *handle* this word intelligently! It's a very interesting word because we're all faced with a myriad of things to handle as we journey through life—and we're generally judged by the way we handle them. As a child I was dubbed a poor sport at times because I couldn't handle losing very well. Fortunately, I haven't been called by that name lately.

Teenage boyfriends called me selfish, my mom said I was self-conscious, and my bandleader pinpointed my shyness. I'm happy to report that I've overcome most of my shyness (I now have to work on not being too obnoxious!) I've also lost a lot of my self-consciousness, especially if I'm motivated by a cause bigger than myself or feel that God's Spirit is leading me. But my selfishness... that's a tough nut to crack. I help others but I have to admit that a lot of my motive is for my own enjoyment, enhancement of my self-image, and others' praise. I now try to do good deeds anonymously when I can. Jesus said to give in secret, expecting nothing in return.

When I was 13 years of age I decided to surprise everyone on Christmas Eve with a gift from "Santa." I purchased little things with each person in mind—a set of salt and pepper shakers for Aunt Florence, a 45 rpm record for my big brother, etc. I also bought something for myself and made a big fuss over it so no one would suspect *me*. I had them totally fooled—and kept the secret for an hour or so! Had I not "let the cat out of the bag" they'd still be wondering!

It's often been said that God won't give us more than we can handle—
whether it's success and blessings or responsibilities and challenges.
With God's help we can handle all of these things wisely and well.

For inspiration, we just need to ask questions like: How did David
handle Goliath? How did Ruth handle her mother-in-law's leaving?
Paul, his imprisonment? And Jesus, death on the cross?

David boldly confronted Goliath; Ruth adopted her mother-in-law's God;
Paul's letters changed the world; and Jesus said: "Your will be done..."
My motto is: I'll handle all things through Christ who strengthens me!
With God's help, all things are possible!

What About You?

1. How well are *you* handling your challenges and successes?

2. What is much too big for you to handle alone?

3. How can God help *you*? And how can you help *others* look to God for help?

Reflect

Ahhh! Finally a word that relaxes me, providing a much-appreciated reprieve from the heavier, soul-searching words. Thank you, Lord! I truly enjoyed reflecting on your many blessings these last few years as I relaxed in our jacuzzi-style tub. I also reflected with gratitude on the many people you have sent into my life to confirm and encourage me. The pastor even mentioned the word *reflect* twice at tonight's Bible Study!

Reflecting is something that has always come easy to me. One of my earliest report cards contains a teacher's note saying that I was doing a lot daydreaming in class and didn't always respond when she spoke to me. It probably didn't help to be called by my nickname, Bam, outside of school—maybe I thought she was speaking to someone else. OK, I know what you're thinking...how did I get the nickname Bam? Much in the same way many nicknames come into being—I started it! As a toddler learning to talk, my rendition of *Ruth Anne* came out as *Bam*. And there are still a few people around who call me by that name!

A forte of mine is thinking about what recently (and sometimes not-so-recently) transpired. I'm very good at bashing myself for having said the wrong thing at the wrong time and/or wishing I'd said something else (or nothing). The good thing about it is that many of the people who thought I wasn't listening eventually discover that I was; I just needed a little pondering time. If their comment inspires an action, I generally move on it—better late than never.

*Jesus reflected, alone with God, as he recharged his spiritual "battery."
We, too, need to reflect to process all the stimuli that bombards us
and reconnect with the Spirit's comfort and understanding.*

*On what should we reflect? God's goodness, our role in his great plan,
how to tap into his power to confront the bad and incorporate the good,
and whatever God communicates as we listen to his still, small voice.*

*Reflection time helps us reflect God's love in our everyday lives.
We can also reflect on, and deepen our concern for, others' welfare,
our love of the Lord, our joy in living each day with purpose/meaning.*

What About You?

1. What do you tend to reflect on?

2. Who do you know who reflects God's love in their lives?

3. How can we brighten the Light in our lives so we can better reflect it
   to others?

Respect

April 22, 2010

Today is Earth Day, a perfect time to respect our natural environment, with its awesome power and fragile vulnerability. Recent earthquakes and a massive volcano eruption in Iceland have displayed a power far stronger than ourselves. But manmade problems resulting from a lack of respect for life (such as the needless slaughter of 23,000 dolphins annually by the Japanese fishermen and pollution of all kinds) are things we can do something about. I emailed the president about the dolphin slaughter and made a donation to the cause through our non-profit.

Our word for today carries with it a certain sadness. Why? Because our world is so full of disrespect today. It seems to me that, because of our ready access to all that's happening, we have lost all constraints—as individuals, as a nation, as a world. A no-holds-barred, let-it-all-hang-out atmosphere seems to prevail. So when I sense some old-fashioned respect (people calling me "Mrs. Tschudin" instead of Ruth, someone holding the door for me, etc.) I really appreciate it.

The Lord's Prayer says "Hallowed be thine name"--a constant reminder that God deserves and demands the respect due to him. He is holy and set apart. And the Scriptures tell us to be holy as he is holy—to set ourselves apart, too. Paul instructed the Roman Christians to:

Love each other as brothers and sisters, and honor others more than you do yourself. Eagerly follow the Holy Spirit and serve the Lord. Be patient in time of trouble and never stop praying. Take care of God's needy people and welcome strangers into your home. Ask God to bless everyone who mistreats you. (some set-us-apart ideas from Romans 12).

Paul says to work hard to earn others' respect, and to live in peace.
We sing "Let there be peace on earth and let it begin with me."
Being kind and respecting others' dignity is a good start.

By being respectful stewards of the flora, fauna, water and air
we can preserve the miracles we see (and often overlook) each day.
Let's recycle, conserve, plant, fight abuses, go green…

Respecting you, dear Lord/Spirit/Jesus, is the most important of all.
How foolish we are to ignore you, take you for granted, and grieve you.
Grant us mercy as we humble ourselves and bow down before you.

What About You?

1. How would you describe the respect level in today's world? What examples come to mind?

2. What can you do to increase the respect level in today's world?

3. What are some other set-us-apart commands from the Gospels and Epistles? What ideas do you have that would give God more respect and glory?

March

April 25, 2010

How do we march on a rainy Sunday? By putting God's commands above our own desires. For me today, it means not sleeping in and missing church, and not begging out of a commitment to walk three miles to benefit homeless families. I hung in there and followed God's marching orders to do both of the above. And I reaped the rewards: seeing my church friends, helping others, and hearing a great sermon on "Coloring Outside the Lines."

The sermon was based on the story in Acts 10 about Peter seeing the visions of the descending sheet containing forbidden animals. God told him to eat the animals, but he refused. Just as God finished explaining why the eating of these animals is acceptable, someone knocked at the door--a servant of Cornelius, a Roman (non-Jewish) centurion. God had spoken to Cornelius and told him to contact Peter. Peter immediately realized the vision's meaning-- that *God shows no partiality; anyone who fears him and does what is right is acceptable to him.*

So Peter "colored outside the lines" and went to Cornelius' house to tell him the Good News. Thanks to Peter's willingness to march to his own "drummer" (the God he loved so much), we are now Christians. And, like Peter, we may sometimes be called to do things we'd rather not do or make changes that may cause problems. But think of John and Peter being ordered to stop their preaching or else bear the dire consequences. Their answer was: *Do you think God wants us to obey you or obey him? We cannot keep quiet about what we have seen and heard. (Acts 4:19-20)*

100

To march is to step out in faith knowing that we're in the palm of God's hand.
We're not promised a rose garden here, but the rewards in heaven far
exceed anything we can ask or imagine. (Eph 3:20, 1 Co 2:9)

Every time I march to your call, Lord, I am amazed at the outcome.
I adopted my dog and wrote a book with her, per your command.
I've held Bible studies, learned Scripture, invited people over.

Here I am writing about today's word because you supplied it.
Even though I'm not sure how this will be used, I happily march!
Please help me discern your orders and march only in your direction.

What About You?

1. What stories can you share about how people (maybe even you, yourself) hear God's call and boldly respond to it?

2. In the Apocrypha's Book of Wisdom (4:12) we're told that *the witchery of paltry things obscures what is right*. What paltry things are attracting marchers nowadays?

3. How can we be confident that we're marching in God's direction and following *his* commands?

Weigh

This certainly isn't my favorite word. It reminds me that a recent weighing on the bathroom scale reveals that I'm heading for the big "150." Some much-needed corrective action is now in the works. Our decision to no longer eat lunch and dinner in front of the television helps immensely—no more mindless snacking while engaged in a TV program. So far it's making a positive difference in a number of ways. And a reminder to weigh in periodically is a wise recommendation in order to stay on top of this common American malady.

The more serious aspect of our word is its connection to measuring and/or contemplating something to be sure it's in balance. The mysterious handwriting on the wall of Babylon's King Belshazzar (See Daniel, chapter 5) was interpreted by Daniel, a Hebrew captive:

> The words written there are mene, which means "numbered," tekel, which means "weighed," and parsin, which means "divided." God has numbered the days of your kingdom and has brought it to an end. He has weighed you on his balance scales, and you fall short of what it takes to be king. So God has divided your kingdom between the Medes and the Persians.

When Jesus noticed the dishonest and unholy practices of the temple money-changers years later, he weighed the situation and then cleared out the merchants and their crooked scales from the temple. He also told a story about the separation of sheep and goats at judgment time (see Matthew 25:31-46)—another example of weighing and balancing things out.

Today I did some of that type of weighing--and acted on my decisions.
I read about the Supreme Court allowing (based on the First Amendment)
the production and sale of videos showing the torture of kittens.

When I weighed this situation in my head and heart, I felt so helpless.
Instead of just feeling badly and doing nothing, I emailed the ASPCA
to shed light on the situation and see what we can do about it.

At bedtime I realized I forgot to contact a newly-widowed friend.
I knew I'd annoy Hugo by doing "just one more thing"… but
I decided in favor of sending a sympathy e-card. He understood.

What About You?

1. Why is it generally best to weigh our thoughts and actions ahead of time? What examples come to mind?

2. What are some Biblical and/or present day examples of the importance of carefully accessing a situation, then doing something about it?

3. Davy Crockett said (accordingly to Walt Disney's depiction of him): "Be sure you're right, then go ahead." When have you followed that advice? How did it work out?

Cry

May 6, 2010

It's odd to have this word crop up in the middle of a beautiful spring day when our baby granddaughter is visiting from Florida (for two whole weeks!) In fact, our days have been so busy that I'm just now (three days later—Sunday, May 9th, Mother's Day) finding time to sit and write about this special word. But because I'm writing it late, I'm seeing it from a more personal perspective. On the 6th it was just an interesting word to contemplate, so my notes point to my thoughts about it. I recalled Jesus weeping at the tomb of Lazarus, showing us that it's a natural thing to do. I also recalled a favorite song that our youth choir sang (under my direction at the time) called "For Those Tears I Died" by Marsha Stevens. The chorus is:

Jesus said, "Come to the water, stand by my side,
I know you are thirsty, you won't be denied;
I felt ev'ry teardrop when in darkness you cried,
And I strove to remind you that for those tears I died."

But today, while watching my granddaughter get baptized (and seeing her parents claim Jesus as Savior while vowing to teach baby Jessica about Jesus) tears of joy filled my eyes. Then, later in the day we went to the cemetery to put flowers on my mother's and grandmother's graves. As I thanked them for loving me so much and passing down a mother-daughter closeness that Elisa and I (and now Elisa and her daughter) are maintaining, I wiped away tears of mixed emotions. Tears are surely God's gift to help us release strong emotions—happy, sad and everything in between. Be they therapeutic tears, tears of desperation and pain, or rejoicing tears, they are a special part of what makes us human--and I praise God for them.

Thanks, Lord Jesus, for inviting us to drink your living water.
We know you feel our pain and hear our heartfelt cries.
You lighten burdens, alleviate guilt, and numb the sting of death.

I pray for compassion to feel others' pain, and help the grieving.
Keep me from callousness and enjoying others' pain, Lord.
Help me to see beyond actions and words to the tears in their hearts.

I pray for those who cry in pain, whose tears are being ignored.
I pray those who cry for joy; may they pass that joy on to others.
I pray for those without you in their lives—may they cry out to you!

What About You?

1. When have you cried happy tears and/or sad ones?

2. When have you cried out to God for help?

3. Whose cries tug at your heartstrings today? Do any cries give you a twinge of pleasure? How, with God's help, can you best respond to both types of cries?

Relinquish

May 9, 2010

Relinquish... a word that tells me it's time to let go of all the excess baggage I've accumulated over the years: things, obligations, emotional garbage, etc. The pastor's sermon today was "Finding Peace with the Past," another reminder that it's time to relinquish all the "stuff" that's weighing me down and holding me back.

I can't help but think of that rich young man who had done everything according to God's will—except for one thing. He held too closely to his riches and "things." (See Mark 19:16-22.) This is the story that leads into Jesus' well-known quote: *It's easier for a camel to go through the eye of a needle than for a rich person to enter the kingdom of God.* That's a scary thought for people in America today, because we are all so "rich" in things.

Recently my hubby and I gave up watching TV. It was taking up a lot of time that could be better spent, and was causing friction between us because I'd keep watching it past our agreed-upon bedtime. I'm so glad we made this decision because I see how much better my life is without a lot of TV.

My Dad used to say that God has a bigger shovel. The more we give (give up), the more good the Lord shovels back at us. We've all heard statements like these: "I volunteer, but the intangible rewards I get back are much more than I give." "My special-needs child has brought more joy into my life than a 'normal' child ever could." "The hardest time in my life is also the best time in my life." "I scaled down my possessions and work hours, and I'm happier than ever!"

Two of my favorite songs refer to relinquishing:
   "I Surrender All" inspires us to place everything in God's hands.
   "Old Rugged Cross" talks of when we lay down our earthly "trophies."

I gladly relinquish (right now) all that hinders me: prideful thoughts,
   hurtful actions, feelings of inferiority. I exchange doubt for faith,
   fear for trust, insecurity for equanimity, rudeness for kindness.

I give up guilt, jealousy, self-centeredness, and boisterousness.
   I relinquish possessions that don't suit your purposes for me, Lord.
   My spirit is willing (at the moment)—but I know I'll need your help.

What About You?

1. Is there anything God is prompting *you* to relinquish?

2. How is it possible to give and end up getting back so much more? (Solomon said: *He who waters will himself be watered.* Jesus said: *Give, and it will given to you good measure, pressed down, shaken together, running over...*)

3. How can relinquishing our loved ones to God be good for all concerned?

Forget

May 11, 2010

Now that I finally sat down to write about our word I forgot what it was! Only when I chided myself for forgetting did I realize that the word itself is *forget*, so I'm excused this time. I forget a lot these days, but for some wonderful reason (hopefully God's blessing on this project) I have thus far been able to easily recall all 131 words-for-the-day thus far—and we're well past our one-third-of-the-year mark, so I expect I will not forget any of the remaining words either.

So, what would God want us to *forget*? Probably wrongs done to us—the way he forgives and forgets when we do wrong: *As far as the east is from the west, so far has He removed our transgressions from us.* (Psalm 103:12)

He probably would also like us to forgive ourselves, and forget those lingering regrets. Whatever we can rectify, great! But whenever I can't make things right, I ask God to do it for me by sending someone else to bless the person I hurt. If the person is deceased, I pray that he or she is at peace and in God's loving hands. I found William P. Young's book *The Shack* to be helpful in this respect because it gives us new perspectives on the tragedies in our lives.

God doesn't even mind if we ask him to remember us. You'll recall that the thief on the cross didn't want to be forgotten. He defended Jesus, then said: *Jesus, remember me when you come into your kingdom* (Luke 23:42). His plea was honored as Jesus, despite his excruciating pain, promptly responded by saying: *Today you will be with me in Paradise.* (See 23:32-43).

We often sing the words of the dying thief as a lead-up to prayer.
Around the campfire we sing "Do Lord, oh do Lord, do remember me."
God doesn't forget us. He knows us each by name and walks with us.

And God even provides some "crutches" to help us not forget him!
The bread and wine/juice (communion) help us recall Jesus' sacrifice.
"Do this in remembrance of me," we're told by Jesus (Lk 22:19).

God's also given us the Holy Spirit to keep us from forgetting.
The Spirit teaches us and helps us recall Jesus' words (Jn 14:26).
With your help, Lord, we'll never forget whose we are--yours, forever.

What About You?

1. Is there anything in *your* past that should be forgotten? What should *not* be forgotten? Why?

2. How can we live our lives so others will be constantly reminded of the God who loves them so?

3. Everything went wrong in Job's life, yet he boldly declared: *I know that my Redeemer lives!* What should we never forget whenever we feel forsaken or in pain?

Meander

Today was a warm, sunny spring day—an ideal day for this lovely word. The computer provides a variety of synonyms but the one I favor most is the one that means *stroll*. I chose this meaning because the word came to me as I taking a relaxing walk with my dog, Jessie, early this evening. We took the time to greet other walkers and *their* canine companions. One couple had three dogs (and cats at home, too). All were taken from unhappy circumstances and now live in a loving home together with this wonderfully compassionate young man and wife.

Surely God wants us to take time to "smell the roses," make new friends, and care for those in need (be they people or animals). Earlier today my daughter and husband were talking about perhaps taking in a foster child and maybe even adopting a child in need. When our daughter was ten years old we welcomed a 5-year-old foster son, Joey, into our home for thirteen amazing months. It's something I feel very good about as I look back on my life from the vantage point of a 65-year-old.

There's so much on my busy agenda, but I will keep this special word in mind when I find myself worried and hurried. We're not meant to rush through life, missing out on the camaraderie, the festivities, the beauty that looks us in the eyes, if we would just take time to appreciate them. These past two weeks I've had to make a number of decisions regarding how to spend my time—should I work on the projects and everyday responsibilities, or should I spend the time enjoying our loved ones who are visiting from Florida?

I made some "meandering" choices lately, Lord. I took my visiting daughter, and baby Jessica to the animal park where we all went on the train ride. I also had a get-together for them and our friends and neighbors.

Jessica was baptized by our new pastor, Chuck Holm. It was lovely. The shawl ministry presented Jessica with a beautiful handmade shawl, lovingly and skillfully crafted by a dear friend, Kathleen McNally.

Our son-in-law went fishing and caught a delicious trout dinner for us. Another evening we ate at a local diner; Jessica (7 mos.) sat with us. I may have put aside other things, Lord, but I know you understand!

What About You?

1. When do (or should) you take time to meander rather than rush?

2. What do you think of my desire to accept as many invitations as I can, write those letters, make those phone calls, and say those intercessory prayers when the thought comes to me, rather than putting them off?

3. Who do you know (or know of) who gets a lot done, yet always seems to have time to help others, honor God, and enjoy life's many blessings? What can we learn from them?

Plant

May 17, 2010

Plant is a great word for this time of year. Our son-in-law, Danny, just planted a variety of lovely flowers, vines, and even a little evergreen tree amid a new layer of peat moss. Our grounds now look totally new and beautiful. We even have a planter with red geraniums and little white flowers hanging from our lamppost, and our backyard shed has vinca and geraniums in its window box. Blossoming flowers now climb up the poles that support our "Florida Room" renovation. What a transformation!

When a group from our church visited the Holy Land in the nineties we stopped at a special nursery where we could purchase young trees and plant them in honor or memory of loved ones. It was such a heartwarming experience as we talked about the loved ones for whom the tree(s) had been planted. And because we did the digging and planted them ourselves it was especially meaningful. It's something I'll never forget.

The word *plant* brings to mind other thoughts, too. For example, I think of the Rev. Dr. Robert Schuller telling his TV viewers to bloom where they are planted. No matter where we are in our life's journey (physically or spiritually) we can make the most of it because God is with us. I love Psalm 139 where David asks, *Where can I flee from your spirit?* Then he goes on to describe the best and worst places—and in all of them he is held by God's victorious right hand. Sunday's sermon by our new Pastor, Chuck Holm, was all about how tightly God holds onto *us*, even when we're too weak or traumatized to hold onto him.

Jesus compared himself to a plant—he, the vine and we, the branches.
Connected to him we grow/flourish; apart from him we can do nothing.
He's the security and nourishment we need for a healthy, happy life.

He sends us to plant seeds of goodness through loving encouragement.
When TV pastor Dr. Schuller was a child, a cherished uncle told him
that one day he'd be a great preacher. The words certainly took root!

Help me, Lord, to plant thoughts of you in people's minds and hearts,
to tear out the weeds of wickedness from my own life, and to
welcome your Spirit into the fertile ground of a humble heart.

What About You?

1. What human transformations can be wrought by well placed "plantings"?

2. Who has planted goodness and confidence in *your* life? How?

3. There are times when one person sows and another reaps. How can the beauty and faith we plant today reap dividends for others down the road?

Reminisce

May 18, 2010

Today was an ideal day to reminisce...cool, dark, drizzly, and no need to even walk the dog (Jessie, our black Lab, hurt her leg, so she rested most of the day). I also spent the better part of the day indoors—going through our daughter Elisa's high school and college mementos, which she was about to discard during her recent visit. I rescued the two bags and one valise filled with cards, letters, photos, and other memorabilia. Amid the crumpled-up notes from one teen to another were some beautiful heartfelt writings by our daughter, then a sensitive young woman finding herself and her path in life. Those and other priceless discoveries are now treasures, saved for her later years.

Elisa had kept every card, postcard, and note she received while living away from home. I hadn't realized that so many wonderful people were so supportive of her. I was surprised to see, for example, that my good friend Ruth Hand Crull (who taught voice and played piano for our children's choir) had sent so many cards to our daughter. Ruth and others have since died, but thoughts of them, and the happy times we shared, warmed my heart. What a vast crowd of Christian witnesses they were—and continue to be. (See Heb 12:1-2.)

Elisa's grandmother (my mom, Grace) sent her almost as many cards and letters as we, her parents, did. Mom excelled in championing Elisa, and Elisa adored her grandmother as one of her all-time heroes. I found a priceless, precious letter that Elisa had written to her deceased grandma just after her death in 1999—a touching tribute to a relationship that was surely made in heaven and will someday be fully restored (also in heaven) by God's grace.

114

We reminisce when we hold God's Scriptures and promises in our hearts.
God's "chosen people" still keep Biblical holidays and traditions.
Christian celebrations and sacraments help us to remember, too.

By looking back to Bible times, and all of human history, we
find strength for today and renewed faith in a caring, forgiving God--
a God who blesses and empowers those who call on his name.

I enjoyed reminiscing, but now it's time to look toward the future.
Jesus said "The harvest is plentiful but the laborers are few." (Lk 10:2)
Let's honor our faith-filled ancestors by being among those laborers!

What About You?

1. What type(s) of reminiscing do you most enjoy?

2. What are some drawbacks of reminiscing? How can they be avoided?

3. How have God and his faithful believers touched your life over the
    years? How does this affect your faith and works today?

Admire

May 22, 2010

This is one of my favorite words. It means to look upon with wonder and delight; to esteem highly. Coveting, on the other hand, means desiring for ourselves whatever it is we're noticing--which can lead to jealousy and self-centered actions.

While walking in the park this morning with Jessie (dog) I couldn't help but admire the colorful bushes in full bloom. They were absolutely lovely! Then I started thinking about what else I admire—in the world and in people. I've always admired my husband, Hugo, for his discipline, strength of character, and sense of humor. And now, after 43 years together, my admiration must have turned to emulation because I've become more like him! I now have the discipline to work in a home office, I'm more likely to stand up for what's right, and I laugh a lot.

I also admire Elisa, our daughter, for her skill at writing, mothering little Jessica, and dealing with people. And I admire our son-in-law for his hard work and love of family. He's very involved in raising our little granddaughter, and he helps Elisa in many different ways.

Inspired by our word-of-the-day, I told Elisa how much I admire her and Danny; and I plan to be much more liberal in telling people when I admire something about them. Hopefully people can admire me, too, perhaps for my creativity or determination. Easiest of all to admire is Jesus—for his obedience to God, his love of people, and his ability to heal, forgive, and save.

Let's find something admirable in all people—and let them know…
and apply those traits to our own lives in creative ways.
Guide us, Lord, in choosing whom to admire and emulate.

I admire: people who use their talents well, the accomplishments of
intelligent and gifted people, congregations that spread God's love,
and those who love others as themselves in healthy, happy ways.

Inspired and masterful architecture, music, and artwork touch my soul
because I admire you most of all, dear maker and lover of our souls.
And my adoration will blossom even more as your great plan unfolds.

What About You?

1. What and whom do *you* admire? Who have been your life-changing role models?

2. Who do you think admires *you*? For what would you most like to be admired?

3. What do you admire most about the nature and works of our amazing three-in-one God?

117

Regret

Regretfully, *regret* is something we all have to deal with. It's certainly been active throughout *my* life. I still recall going to the little neighborhood grocery store as a child and filling my little brown bag with an extra malted milk ball. At two for a penny I should have taken ten for my nickel, but I purposely took 11. I knew that the owner, a friend of our family, would trust me. And if he *did* check my count, it would look like an honest error. But God and I knew the truth, which for almost 60 years has been a shame I've had to live with.

While making the bed this morning I thought of another incident that happened almost 50 years ago—something I didn't think much about at the time. My college roommate and I were making fun of a heartfelt poem a young man we both knew had written to, and about, her. Looking at it now from a distance, I realize what a nasty thing we'd done, even though only the two of us even knew about it. Yes, Lord, even these subtle sins evoke regret. I see why you sent us this word--the more we think about our past the more regrets float into our consciousness.

I've always thought that regret is a bad thing—something to be acknowledged, confessed, forgiven, and forgotten. Surely if it's not dealt with in this manner, it could adversely affect our present and future. But as today unfolded I started to look at it from a new perspective. Maybe regret is something good, too. Look at St. Paul. In Romans 7:14-25 he laments about his many regrets—doing that which he knows is wrong. He says, "What a miserable person I am. Who will rescue me…? Thank God, Jesus Christ will rescue me!"

Paul shares his regrets so we realize that he needs forgiveness, too.
Regret unites us as humans, making us more compassionate and aware
that we need a Savior to forgive and guide us in a better direction.

I regret, Lord, that I wasn't always kind to my sister growing up.
I've mistreated friends—and was absolutely horrible to boyfriends.
And I wish I'd been more thankful, helpful, and loving to my parents.

As a tourist I was once very unchristian toward a poor street vendor,
I wish I'd been a better mother… friend… follower of Christ…
But praise God, it's a new day and my regrets are in his loving hands.

What About You?

1. As you ponder your past, what regrets (expected and unexpected) surface?

2. What regrets are you still holding onto that should be handed over to God for forgiveness and redirection?

3. What are some examples of regrets being turned into service for God and others?

Forge

May 25, 2010

The chosen meaning for today's word is "to move forward steadily." The dictionary notes that it's often used in connection with the word *ahead*. So, I'll now *forge ahead* by giving our word-of-the-day the thought and attention it deserves! It's a word that connotes, to me, a determined movement in spite of challenges and hardships. For example, I can well imagine a person on a dogsled forging ahead in a blizzard, the early Christian church forging ahead despite persecution, and a newly widowed person forging head to get through each painful day.

Today, I forged ahead with my new 3-part "to-do" list, which is already simplified into 1, 2, and 3-level tasks rather the original designations of critical, important and nice. The numbers mean the same; it's just an easier way to think of them. And I'm pleased to report that even though I took two naps, two dog walks, and made two well-balanced meals, I was able to knock off 5 of the 6 tasks in column number 1, and even a couple from column number 2.

I also went to the final meeting of the spring Bible Study at church. We've been discussing change. It's very interesting because we all have to deal with change. In fact, it's a major factor in our lives. Tonight we discussed the future and where we expect to be in ten years, our greatest fear about the end of our lives, the thoughts expressed in Psalm 139, and how God and Jesus are our Rocks. The bottom line was that the only certainties in our lives are Jesus Christ and change. Knowing that, it's easier to forge ahead, isn't it?

There are wonderful Biblical examples of people who have forged ahead:
Jacob wrestled for a blessing and his name became Israel (Gen 2:24-32);
Ruth's love of mother-in-law brought her into a whole new life.

David's penitence and humble attitude kept him going (2 Sam 11 and 12);
Paul didn't let persecution and hardship keep him from his mission;
and Jesus forged ahead despite the excruciating death awaiting him.

Help us to forge ahead in our lives, too, Lord. Go before us to show
the way, behind us to encourage us, beside us to befriend us, above
us to watch over us, and within us to give us peace (Pastor Chuck).

What About You?

1. When were you able to forge ahead with something on your own? With someone's help? With God's help?

2. Who do you know (of know of) who's a good example of forging ahead?

3. They say that fools rush in where angels fear to tread. When can forging ahead be problematic?

Survey

May 26, 2010

It's funny (odd) that I've always had an interest in survey results—and even in doing my own surveys. I recall, as an elementary school sixth-grader, asking my classmates their religion, their political bent, and other personal questions; then I tallied the results--just for the fun of it! What nerve--especially for a shy kid like me! In college I surveyed my classmates again (different ones, of course—all were future teachers). This time I asked questions about their reactions to teacher-made tests and based my term paper on their responses.

After my first year of teaching I earned graduate credits while touring Europe. It was a trip organized by one of the state teacher's colleges. We were asked to write a paper about something relevant to the trip (I wrote about how foreign languages studied in school were being put to good use.) We were also given a few questions to ask locals we encountered. So here I was, once again surveying people. It was a little more challenging this time because we had to find locals who spoke English (in 1966) and had to question them about things I knew very little about (like the possibility of a European union). But I asked the locals--and all my traveling companions--about their use of foreign languages studied, which made my paper very interesting.

After nine years of teaching, I was at it again! I was given a full-year's sabbatical leave with half pay--to write a book to help teachers. For this project I designed questions about everything I could think of relating to teaching. Hundreds of teachers took part—specially selected outstanding teachers and also a control group of randomly selected teachers. More than 80 statistically significant differences surfaced and were discussed on TVs "Today Show."

The book that most influenced the best teachers was the Bible.
Great teachers tended to be more involved in religious activities.
All of the survey results were published in book form in 1980.

Much later, in the late 90's, I took a Christian Counseling course and
surveyed a sampling of pastors for a research paper I was writing.
I was amazed at how many pastors I knew well enough to involve.

Now, I've given up surveying people so I can concentrate on you, Lord.
And, as the hymn by Isaac Watts says: "When I survey the wondrous
cross... love so amazing demands my soul, my life, my all."

What About You?

1.   What "surveying" have you done in the past?

2.   In what ways can we survey (learn from and about) God?
     What questions would you like to ask him?

3.   If God were to tally the results of his survey of us, how would we do?
     What questions do you think he would ask us, and how would he help
     us move forward based on the survey results?

Invest

May 29, 2010

When we think of it, we're all in the investing business, aren't we? We generally think of investing our money, but we also invest our time, our energy, our hopes, and our dreams—in all sorts of people, places, and things. Sometimes we invest so much of ourselves in an endeavor that we seem to let go even though we know we should. That old Rock'n'Roll favorite, "Breaking Up is Hard to Do," describes just such a difficult time and decision.

My parents are my shining examples when it comes to handling investments well. They'd be shocked to hear this because they never had much of a savings account. Yet they died rich—in loved ones and good deeds. In their younger years Dad enjoyed learning, wearing snazzy clothes and driving sporty cars, and Mom enjoyed playing the piano, writing stories, and sketching fashions. Dad chose to marry and start a business (*Howard's Cleaners and Dyers*) rather than go to college, and Mom gave up her dreams to help him and to raise three children. They invested in us instead of themselves and today we are all hard workers and faithful Christians, thanks mostly to them.

They were also good examples when it came to enjoying material things, yet letting go without a whimper when the time came. Mom gave up her engagement ring when her brother returned from World War II and couldn't afford a ring for his war bride. Dad gave up his business when skunks burrowed beneath his store, and they both agreed to sell our home after we "kids" were married and on our own. Dad was also a smoker at a time when the risks weren't revealed. But once the doctor told him to quit, he just threw his open pack away and stopped "cold turkey."

My parents also invested in their faith by attending church regularly.
Over the years Mom taught Sunday School and Vacation Bible School;
Dad sang in the choir and worked on various church committees.

Dad said, "You can't out-give the Lord; God has a bigger shovel."
We never had excess, but we had bicycles, cars, college, pets, love...
Dad often said, "The Lord will provide," and he was never disappointed.

Dad died at home at age 76; Mom was hospitalized only to give birth. She
said she didn't think death would be difficult—at 88 she died at home.
I look forward to seeing them again soon. I, too, invest in faith.

What About You?

1.   In Matthew 6:19-21 Jesus tells us to build up treasures in heaven. How are you following his advice?

2.   What are some other ways to add to our treasures-in-heaven accounts?

3.   In Matthew 13:44-46 Jesus compares the Kingdom of Heaven to people who find something so valuable they sell/sacrifice everything to purchase it. What is the "pearl of great price" in *your* life?

Pause

May 31, 2010

Today is Memorial Day the finishing touch to a weekend of fair weather, which was great for picnics, parades, swimming...you name it. Today's word reminds me, however, that the purpose of this holiday is not for our recreation, but to give us *pause* to remember and honor those who gave their all for our freedom. Earlier in the weekend I combined Jessie's walk with watching our local parade. And last evening, Hugo and I watched the National Washington DC Memorial Day Concert on television--it was wonderful, with well-known singers and actors inspiring us and telling us about the wars Americans have fought in over the years. I hadn't realized how many of our people were killed or wounded in these wars. What a great sacrifice on behalf of so many...

Today I did something I haven't done in years—I fasted. Not a liquid-free "complete" fast as I did in my younger years, but a food-only fast. I've always combined my daylong fasts with special purposes and prayers, which I think about and act on each time I feel a hunger pang. Today's purposeful prayer is threefold: for our country to turn to God in repentance and faith; for the families of those who lost their lives in defense of our country; and for veterans who live with broken bodies and torturous memories. I also pause to thank God for our country, for our freedom, and for those brave people whose lives were cut short to protect these blessings. I envision these heroes and heroines whole and fulfilled, in the palm of God's hand.

May we never take for granted all that we enjoy today, thanks to these brave people. May we pause often to remember, and then pledge to live our lives worthy of such sacrifice.

126

We see the rows of crosses at cemeteries all over the world.
  We scan the names on monuments and know we're on sacred ground.
    Only you, dear Lord, can sort it all out and apply a healing balm.

We see photographs of the "collateral damage"—innocent victims of war.
  We imagine the horror they experienced and the lives they missed.
    Only you, dear Lord, can reach down deep enough to make things right.

Kyle, a young soldier from our church, died in Iraq. His family still mourns.
  I'm ashamed of how lightly I've regarded fallen heroes in the past.
    Only you, dear Lord, can mold us into all we can and should be.

What About You?

1.   What in *your* life needs some extra pause and prayer?

2.   Psalm 46:10 tells us to *Be still and know that I am God.* How can
     a pause for this type of silence make a difference in our lives?

3.   What can we do to ease some of the pain in today's world?

Discover

June 5, 2010

Most of our words appear at the start of the day (like manna from Heaven). Some appear a day ahead (like the double manna that the Israelites collected the day *before* the Sabbath, so they could rest on the Sabbath and not have to gather the food). But the word *discover* was quite unusual because *it* (and a couple of others) came to me earlier than usual, so I just slated them ahead. And, as so often happens, this particular word ended up being the perfect word for its day.

On an early morning dog walk I asked the Lord to help me discover some valuable things today—perhaps about others... or myself... or *him*! But instead, he surprised me by sending an unexpected discovery my way: a simple system to help me better handle all the tasks related to my two big projects, the August fundraiser for our foundation and the Amazon Book Launch in September. Each of these projects entails a plethora of small tasks, all of which need to be attended to in order to have a successful event.

Earlier this week I thought I'd found a good system: a way of categorizing the tasks as critical, important, or just nice to do. But this new approach makes it even easier and more efficient. I now categorize my tasks by project, with a third category called "Other" (anything that isn't related to the big projects). I no longer write my things-to-remember onto papers, which I tend to lose. Instead, I whip them onto my computerized list, so I only have to enter them once, have immediate access, and can enter and delete items at record pace. To many, this is so obvious and commonplace—and I knew *about* it...but today I discovered how well it works!

I did a lot today, Lord, and felt quite in control. What a relief!
I know that together you and I can handle these current projects,
and whatever else may come my way as I travel through life.

As long as I'm close to you I know there will be new discoveries
to guide and bless me in ways I can only begin to imagine.
I won't fear the future, Lord—I'll embrace it!

Today I helped someone, encouraged a widow, went on a walk with Hugo.
I lavished in the jacuzzi tub, relaxed on the patio, and spoke to you.
Now I'll retire for the night, thanking and loving you wholeheartedly.

What About You?

1. Just imagine how surprised the Israelites were when they first saw the manna. What surprising discoveries or revelations have *you* had in *your* life?

2. What have been some of the best (and worst) discoveries people have made over the years? How is it possible for a discovery to be both good *and* bad?

3. How can we discover more about the God who loves us and is ready to help us with all our needs and desires?

Whisper

June 6, 2010

A quiet morning walk before church inspired today's word. And what a great word it is! The area in which we've been living for the past 36 years is more stressful, noisy, and hectic than many other areas of our state, country, and world. But we love our house because it's close to the action, yet it's on a quiet dead-end street with a river behind it, and a borrowed woodsy view (protected water-company property) beyond the river. It's so nice to sit quietly on the back patio and just listen to the birds and the wonderful sounds of nature that so often get blocked out.

When we toured the Mormon Tabernacle in Salt Lake City, Utah, many years ago they demonstrated how the acoustics were so fine-tuned that a pin dropping or a whispering person facing away from the audience could be clearly heard throughout the huge sanctuary. It was amazing. But even more amazing is the fact that God hears our little whispers no matter where we are in relation to him. Greater still is the fact that when we switch from whispering to listening, we are likely to hear God whispering to us!

Elijah was a prophet of the Lord who went through a really hectic time. He challenged 450 false prophets to a contest of faith (then did away with them), climbed Mt. Carmel to usher in the much-needed rain, outran a racing chariot, and then fled from Jezebel who vowed to kill him. Not surprisingly, he was so exhausted and depressed when he finally sat down to rest, he begged God to let him die. Instead, God sent him food and drink via an angel so he'd have enough strength for the 40-day walk that lay before him. For the whole story See 1 Kings 18:1-19:18.

130

When Elijah got to Mt. Sinai God paid him a personal visit.
He met God...not in the wind, the earthquake, or the fire, but in the
gentle breeze that ushered in the still, small voice—the whisper!

Whispers are powerful—they can be divisive, malicious, and damaging.
They can also express understanding, compassion, and rare communication
like we see in the work done by the horse and dog whisperers.

A well-known hymn says to whisper prayers morning, noon, and night.
'Twill keep our hearts in tune—so we can experience God's voice and
the "Whispering Hope" he sends our way when we need it the most.

What About You?

1. When has a human whisper angered or upset you? Comforted or encouraged you?

2. When did a whisper from God help or inspire you?

3. Elijah was rewarded with the most triumphant and unique of deaths (2 K 2:1-18). What unexpected blessings have you and others experienced?

Seize

June 8, 2010

Let's seize this opportunity to let the adventurer in each of us come to the fore. For Hugo and me it was a real "Carpe diem!" day. This phrase was first written in a Latin poem by Horace, but it was popularized by Robin Williams in the movie, "Dead Poet's Society." In this positive context it means to *seize the day*—to enjoy it and make use of it. And that's what we did! It was a beautiful spring day, so we drove to one of our favorite places, Ocean Grove, a quaint old Methodist town bordering the Atlantic Ocean. We enjoyed a hearty meal at a Chinese Buffet and then a lovely stroll on the boardwalk. If that's not seizing the day, I don't know what is!

There's something about this word, however, that makes me think of an impetuosity that says "There it is—let's *seize* it before it disappears." Maybe I'm thinking this way because I'm prone to hasty decisions. I married Hugo hardly knowing him. We met in late April and married in November. He lived in NYC and I lived on the other side of the George Washington Bridge, in NJ, so seeing each other was a bit of a hassle. We met at a Swiss dance in the city, which I attended with Lois, a Swiss friend and fellow teacher. I liked Hugo's openness and honesty; he made sure I knew that he was going through a divorce, was 14 years older than me, and wasn't very religious—in fact, he considered himself an agnostic.

A friend pointed out the Scripture about not being unequally yoked with a non-believer (2 Co 6:14), so I knew this was not God's perfect will, but something (or Someone) deep within encouraged me to go ahead anyway.

*This year we'll celebrate our 43rd anniversary; God has certainly blessed us.
We've had ups and downs: a miscarriage, my running home to mother once,
countless joys, and a consistent effort to keep God in the our lives.*

*Billy Graham often quoted 2 Co 6:2: "Now is the day of salvation!"
and Jesus stressed the need to be alert and ready, so there are
times of importance and urgency when we must seize the opportunity.*

*Some of the opportunities I've seized were total disasters; others far
exceeded my expectations; many brought me closer to you, Lord.
Please show me the way so I can cease or seize according to your will.*

What About You?

1. When have *you* "seized" the day and been glad (or not so glad) you
    did?"

2. What are some examples of opportunities that should definitely be
    passed by? ...carefully pondered or researched? ....seized
    immediately?

3. Luke 19:1-10 tells how Zacchaeus dramatically seized a very
    important opportunity. What opportunities does God offer us today
    that inspire a Zacchaeus-like response?

Glide

Our friend Heiner was an amateur glider pilot. He also flew small motorized planes, but he preferred the glider because of the joy and freedom it afforded him as he silently soared through the skies. It seems so effortless to be gliding along—and it is, as long as someone skillful is piloting. In 2009 a US Air pilot known as "Sully" Sullenberger executed a dramatic landing of a jet-turned-glider when its motor conked out. Because of God's grace, and Sully's glider experience, the plane with more than 150 people aboard landed safely in the Hudson River. Then, thanks to heroic efforts of rescuers who rushed to help, everyone lived to tell about it.

Sometimes we need to purposely relax and put our lives on "glide" for a while. Then, like Heiner, we'll enjoy this smoother, quieter time in comparison to the noisier, energy-guzzling alternative. When we work hard and play hard day in and day out, we can get so stressed that our well-being suffers. A switch from our barreling-along mode to a gliding-along mode can work wonders in preventing and treating the many stress-related side effects of our modern-day living.

Other times, similar to Sully's situation, we might find ourselves suddenly and unexpectedly without the motor we've always depended on, and are forced to glide along on our own momentum. We may fear a crash landing because we've never been in such a dangerous position before. That's when we have to "go with the glide" and let the master Pilot take over for us. The well-known "Footprints in the Sand" poem by Mary Stevenson talks about God carrying us during the most difficult times in our lives—we glide, God pilots.

"Jesus, Savior, Pilot Me" has been sung for over a hundred years,
comforting and inspiring countless people.
The song ends with Jesus saying "Fear not, I will pilot you."

Thank you, Lord, for giving us your Son to be the captain of our lives.
With him steering, we can shut down our sputtering motors and
glide right through the storms and challenges of life.

But we can't just sit back--we still have to do our part.
Check out the Web site www.promiseofgod.com/bikeride/
to see how life compares to a bike ride with Jesus!

What About You?

1. When do you most need a refreshing, therapeutic, take-a-glide time?
    What type of respite do you prefer?

2. When was your life forced into a paralyzing glide by situations
    beyond your control? How did you find your way to a safe landing?

3. Why is it wise to let Jesus pilot us at *all* times?

Diversify

June 12, 2010

They say that variety is the spice of life—and now, more than ever before, we can live a rich, varied life. True, we have horrendous challenges, but we also have access to more knowledge and opportunity than our ancestors could ever have imagined.

Looking back, I see that I've been blessed with a very diversified life. My brother, sister, and I grew up near both a school playground and a park. We made our own fun—with kids of all ages to share it with. If we weren't biking, we were locking skates onto our shoes or playing baseball. On a rainy day, we'd play school, canasta, *Easy Money*—or watch Charlie Chan on TV.

In college I studied to be an elementary school teacher, enjoying still more diversity. I studied all kinds of subjects: astronomy, child psychology, music (played sax in the band), speech, you name it! And my nine years as a teacher were never boring—there were always new things to do. One year we had a workbench and sewing machine in our classroom, thanks to a Technology for Children program; we even put together lamps that actually worked!

Then I married a Swiss man (Hugo), did a lot of travel, and enjoyed raising our daughter while working in his international marketing firm. I got great exposure to finance, customer service, marketing, and management. And now, in my "golden years" I'm still learning as I create brochures and slide shows, write books and press releases, oversee our charitable non-profit, plan big events, and keep financial records for our foundation, C-Corp, family trust, and us personally.

Help me, Lord, to use my time on this earth in ways that please you.
Show me when to diversify and when to "stick to my knitting."
Open my heart and mind to new ideas and possibilities.

I've tried the things that interest me, like traveling and real-estate.
I've given the clarinet, piano, and singing a go—with varying results.
And I've gained much from books, tapes, and evening classes.

My greatest joy over the years has been writing, and it still is.
Lead me where you will, Lord. Might I suggest some creative innovations
in my writing that will touch people's lives and glorify you?

What About You?

1. How diversified has *your* life been?

2. What are you most interested in? How might you diversify in that area?

3. What are some examples of God-pleasing diversification?

Serve

June 14, 2010

It's human nature to prefer *being* served to *doing* the serving. Mark tells us that two disciples (James and John) asked Jesus to let them sit with him, one at his right side and the other at his left, when his time of glory comes. Matthew's Gospel says it was their mother who approached Jesus, but either way, the answer was the same: *God the Father will decide, not me*. Of course the other disciples were angry when they heard about the incident, but Jesus gathered them together and stressed the lesson: *If you want to be great you must be the servant of all the others.* (Mark 10:43) Another time (Mark 9:35), when the disciples were arguing about who was the greatest, Jesus told them again: *If you want the place of honor, you must become a slave and serve others.*

The message is clear: even though people vie (and die) for power and wealth, it's better to serve than be served. And, *It's more blessed to give than receive (Paul quoting Jesus in Acts 20:35)*. Serving is actually a giving of ourselves (our time and talents), rather than giving from the abundance of our possessions. I don't enjoy preparing the coffee for church events, for example, so I don't volunteer to do it. But when those of us in the church Bible Study take turns doing it, I do my part—and usually end up enjoying it a lot more than I thought I would! The most powerful type of serving is, of course, the hard work of on-going sacrifices for a higher good. That's why we say that those who jeopardize their lives for our freedom are *serving* our country—and animals trained to help people are called *service* animals.

Serving God and others can be hard, but the rewards are priceless. People often say that they get back much more than they give. Their service is "bread upon the waters" (Ec 11:1), returning good to them.

Brother Lawrence, a 17th century monk, wrote "The Practice of the Presence of God." He found great joy even in peeling potatoes, because God was near. He found God's presence in all places and situations.

Help me, Lord, to have the heart of a servant, unselfish and giving. May I serve you and others in countless ways: by persevering, forgiving, encouraging, loving—and enjoying you and them.

What About You?

1. In what ways do *you* enjoy serving? How can serving in not-so-enjoyable ways be a growth experience for those who serve?

2. What are some unexpected paybacks you've received because you chose to serve?

3. In Colossians 3:23 Paul says to work willingly as if serving the Lord himself. Who do you know who does this?

Call

June 18, 2010

The Psalmist says that *The Lord is my shepherd*...and *We are the sheep of his pasture.* Jesus says in John 10 that he knows his own sheep and he calls them by name; they hear his voice and follow him. He explains that he then leads them and gives them eternal life; they will never perish and no one can snatch them away from him. Both Peter and Paul follow up by quoting a statement made by the prophet Joel: *All who call upon the name of the Lord shall be saved (See Acts 2:14-16: Peter's speech at Pentecost; Paul's letter to the Romans 10:13; and Joel 2:28-32.).*

My dad used to joke around by saying, "You can call me whatever you want to—just don't call me late for dinner!" For generations, children have chanted: "Sticks and stones will break my bones, but names will never hurt me." But we all know that the emotional scars caused by name-calling can be far worse than physical scars. What and *to what* we are called affect us in powerful ways. It's an amazing gift we've been given: to be assured via the Scriptures that those of us who love and follow Jesus are called Children of God, called by name to share in a secure and everlasting union with him and the God of the universe who created us.

The best way to come to God is to listen for Jesus' voice, and then follow him. What an incredible life we can then live! But even those who miss out on that greatest of joys have hope. A loving God reminds us that it's never the wrong time or place to call on his name. Joel, Peter and Paul each proclaimed the same thing under varying circumstances: that all who sincerely call out to God will be heard and saved, much like the dying thief who called out to Jesus.

Isn't it amazing how we can call almost anywhere by cell phone?
And we can pretty much "call the shots" on all our decisions.
But the most important call we can make is to God.

I call your name often, don't I, Lord? Thanks for not tiring of me.
I call when I have emergencies and huge needs, and I don't hesitate
to call on you with smaller concerns. And when all's well.

I call to you when I awake, and throughout the day I seek you: as I
read your Word, go for a walk, ask your blessing on our meals, and
wind up the day at the kneeling bench in my "Inspiration Room."

What About You?

1. Do you have a private place, similar to my Inspiration Room, that provides a peaceful setting for listening and speaking to the Lord? Why is it important not to limit our connection to God to just special times and/or places?

2. To what do you feel *called*?

3. God called out "Samuel, Samuel!" A little boy responded, and now two Books of the Bible are named for him. What other examples can you give of people (in either biblical times or our own times) who have responded to a call from God or Jesus?

Eat

June 19, 2010

This short word carries with it a lot of emotional baggage, doesn't it? Food has always been more than just a necessary source of physical nourishment—it's a way to bring people together. In biblical times hospitality was not just a social grace, but a moral duty. God's chosen people were told to entertain strangers passing through, even if those strangers were considered enemies. Abraham and Sarah fed God's messengers, who told them that they'd soon have a baby despite their advanced ages (Genesis 18:1-14); and Jacob used food to deceive his father and steal his older brother's birthright in Genesis, chapter 27.

Jesus attended weddings and banquets, and had followers and friends who cooked for him. He even prepared a fish-fry for his disciples (John 21:1-14). He multiplied food when necessary and even used food (bread and wine) to remind us of what his crucifixion was all about. In Revelation 3:20 he says, *Listen! I am standing and knocking at your door. If you hear my voice and open the door, I will come in and we will eat together.* Eating is, indeed, a gift from God.

But in today's affluent society the word "eat" can be a four-letter word to many. The over-abundance and availability of so much food—both healthy and unhealthy—and the use of unhealthy food to celebrate, comfort, and reward... have resulted in health disorders such as obesity, diabetes, anorexia, and bulimia. More people than ever are ruining their lives and over-taxing our health-care system (and economy) because of their eating habits. I, too, am guilty of eating too much, too fast--and succumbing to unhealthy treats for the wrong reasons.

It's definitely time to look seriously at my eating habits.
I eat good food—organic, whenever it's possible and affordable. But
my love of sugar and processed treats are my downfall.

Please help me, Lord, to get and keep this part of my life under better control.
Instead of indulging myself, I'll invite people over here for a meal.
I'll entertain strangers and perhaps some angels! (See He 13:2.)

When I think of those dying of starvation, whose cupboards are bare,
I'm ashamed of myself... yet here I am ordering out for Chinese food.
Jesus, I'm opening the door—please come and eat with me. I need you.

What About You?

1. What mixed emotions do *you* carry in regard to food? What are the pros and cons of your eating habits?

2. What can we do for ourselves, and others, to encourage eating as God intended it?

3. In what ways can we open the door and "eat" with Jesus? (See Rev 3:20)

Recruit

As usual, our chosen word somehow worked its way into my daily activities. This time it even hit me from two directions: I *did* some recruiting, and I *was* recruited. The recruiting I did involved getting a Web designer from Elance to help with our Dogfest Internet site. Dogfest is a big fundraising event our foundation has each year and Elance is a great site that saves us time, work, and money by doing the recruiting for us. We just post an ad for what we want, and professional freelancers from all over the world respond and bid on the job.

I also worked on a press release for Dogfest that included some recruiting. First, I tried to make the article as attractive as I could, so people would read it. I took dog photos from our last Dogfest and had the dogs saying humorous things to entice people to come *this* year. Then I ended by trying to recruit some volunteers to help during the event. That type of recruiting is difficult—everybody's so busy and no one wants to work for free. So, I had to "sell" them on it by saying it's a great way for people who love dogs (but don't have any of their own) to show their support and be part of the festivities. I referred to them as Dogfest Angels and promised a surprise gift for each at our pre-event meeting. Time will tell if my recruiting approach works...

After all this recruiting, I suddenly found myself being the "recruitee." I got two emails regarding dogs in need of homes, which I forwarded on to my database of animal rescue groups. And I also got an email about a judge deciding the fate of a dog; they needed folks to stand on the side of the dog—so I joined the group and sent in my plea for mercy.

I'm dog-tired, for sure! But I truly believe what I was quoted as saying:
"When we help animals, we help people…because animals help us!"
They're a precious gift from you, Lord. Help us to enjoy and protect them.

Thanks for recruiting our foundation Open Doors to help both people
and animals. It's an honor and privilege to have an organization
that does your work and points people in your direction.

Jesus recruited ordinary people and made them extraordinary.
He can make our ordinary lives extraordinary, too.
Help us, Lord, to become living testaments to your love and goodness.

What About You?

1. What work do you think God has waiting just for you? What work are you already doing for and with God?

2. What are some examples that come to mind of people who have become extraordinary because of they were recruited and changed by God?

3. In what ways do you feel like a recruiter, and in what ways do you feel like a recruitee?

Compromise

Nobody likes to be in a compromising position, but like it or not, that's exactly where we sometimes find ourselves—more often than we realize. When Hugo and I married almost 43 years ago we knew we were in for some compromises, especially in the faith category. I was a firm believer and he was adamant doubter—which is where we both still stand after all this time. But I know down deep that Hugo has learned a lot from my God-centered activities (and our in-house prayer, Bible reading and discussions). He's definitely closer to God than he thinks he is. And a wise pastor once told us that we're not as far apart on this issue as we think we are.

Looking back at our 43 years I realize there have been more compromises than expected. Hugo, especially, earns a crown for living with our pets for so many years. He likes them but he doesn't think the compromises are worth it—like our not being able to vacation as much as we'd like because of the unique needs of Annabelle and Jessie. Yet Hugo is behind me 100% and helps a lot with my charity work on behalf of animals who need loving homes.

In order to get along with others we *have* to compromise once in awhile. That's what peacemaking is all about. We just have to think ahead and decide what we'll compromise on and what we won't. Compromising our values is never a good choice, no matter how tempting it may be. That type of compromising is what Hugo (my "agnostic") calls "compromising with the devil." Just today, in Proverbs, I read this: *Can a man take fire to his bosom and his garments not be burned? Or can a man walk on live coals, and his feet not be scorched?* (6:27-28)

*Keep me, Lord, from giving in, even a little, to the devil's devious ways.
Jesus protected himself with Scripture. When the devil slyly quoted
Scripture, too, Jesus heaped still more Scripture on him! (Mt 4:1-11)*

*Help me to gladly compromise when it helps another or glorifies you, Lord.
When in doubt, remind me, dear Spirit, to ask your opinion.
Help me, Lord Jesus, to follow your example and know the Bible well.*

*It's tempting to quit or take short cuts when we're stressed,
tired, bored, frustrated, etc. I pray often for wisdom and discernment
to make good decisions for God's glory in our shades-of-gray world.*

What About You?

1. What examples can you cite of people compromising with the devil and getting "burned?"

2. When have you compromised and been glad (or not so glad) you did? Who has made a lot of compromises for *your* sake?

3. What are some tricks the devil uses on *you*? What Scriptures do you find helpful when you're tempted to go in the wrong direction?

Soften

June 26, 2010

People with smiles on their faces and kindness in their eyes are God's gift to a world filled with bumps and bruises. I, for one, am naturally drawn to people who remind me of loved ones—or of a loving God. Amid Hugo's many Swiss relatives (his mom was one of fifteen children) there was one aunt I hugged the moment I met her. People were no doubt wondering why—I was, too. Then I realized that she reminded me of my Aunt Grace here in the States.

Adding softness to the world is something I definitely want to do. But before I can do that I have to soften myself. I may be enthusiastic (and that's good), but I also tend to be abrupt, harsh, indiscreet, boisterous, and overbearing. See how harsh I can be! And it doesn't help to have those notorious deep wrinkles that go from my nose to the sides of my mouth. I look like Miss Hannigan in the "Annie" movie. I could sure use a facelift, but folks who do that often end up with a tight-looking mouth, which is just as bad.

I'm sure my appearance would soften (wrinkles and all) if I were to soften my thoughts, words, and actions. They definitely need a divine makeover, but God needs something to work with—perhaps a softer attitude toward myself would be a good place to start. I should give myself a break more often and not take myself too seriously. And having a kinder, gentler picture of God is another step in the softening process. Dr. Phil says we all need a soft place to land, and by softening our perception of who we are and the God who made us who we are, we're building that soft place—something that will benefit us and the others we attract.

Sometimes we don't realize how we look and sound to others—that
what people remember about us is generally how we made them feel.
When we're attuned to others' feelings we won't be so abrasive.

My mom alerted me when I was speaking too harshly to my growing child.
Parents may love their children, but the children don't always know it.
I want to speak with an inner softness that can't be misunderstood.

Proverbs 15:1 says that a soft answer turns away wrath.
Help us to be the grease, the cartilage, the velvet glove…
that gets us and others through the "rocks and hard places" of life.

What About You?

1. What does "an iron fist in a velvet glove" mean to you? What are some good examples?

2. What are some things we can do to soften our outlook and our actions?

3. When did Jesus exude a softness? When was he an iron fist, with or without the velvet glove?

Sigh

June 27, 2010

As far as I can see, there are three kinds of sighs:
* a sigh that says "Whew! What a relief! Thank heaven!"
  * a sigh that says "Oh no! Not *that* again! What a burden!"
    * a sigh that says "Ahhhh! It doesn't get any better—this is heaven!"

Upon awakening this morning I breathed the first type of sigh, saying to myself, "TGIS: Thank God it's Sunday! What a joyful relief to have a day where I don't have to feel pressured to work on everyday projects, a day to draw closer to God in my own special way." During church, I felt like exhaling a sigh of annoyance when the visiting pastor (while ours is on vacation) clouded his otherwise great sermon by introducing a controversial topic. Later, I enjoyed a delightful sigh of ecstasy when Hugo and I made passionate love—a real blessing at ages 81 and 66.

A story I recently read on the Internet tells of a little girl looking for a puppy. Her parents kept bringing her to shelters and rescue groups whenever puppies were available. But time after time she'd nestle a puppy, only to declare, "Not this one!" When asked why not, she'd simply say it wasn't the right size. The day finally came when she picked up a puppy and joyfully exclaimed, "Here he is! He's just right." Her parents asked why this one particular puppy was so special. The little girl explained that the puppy had sighed contentedly as soon as she held him—the way her parents sigh and hug each other after being apart for a while. Yes, his *sighs* fit perfectly!

150

You know my sighs well, Lord. Some are heartfelt; most are habit.
I sigh when I sit down, get out of the car, or anticipate a task…
Hugo's told me not to sigh so much—I guess you've noticed it, too.

Help me not to exaggerate or over-dramatize. Let my sighs be genuine.
May they be "just the right sighs" for edifying and helping;
too many negative ones drag me down and chase others away.

Help me eradicate resigning, critical, exasperated, impatient sighs--
to be replaced by praise, cheerfulness, and a kind, uplifting word.
Together we can do this, Lord! [Sigh! of contentment]

What About You?

1. When have you used these three kinds of sighs?

2. What other kind(s) can *you* think of?

3. Which Bible characters sighed—or deserve to have sighed? Why?

Entertain

June 28, 2010

Our word today conjures up lots of good feelings. We all like to entertain and/or *be* entertained! Hugo and I haven't had much time to entertain lately, but with our new "Sabbath set-apart" we look forward to being a little more sociable. Today (not even a Sunday) I made time for "old" friends that go *way* back—to our formative years when we attended the same school and church. I invited them here (despite the condition of our house), but we ended up meeting midway--at a diner. We had a great time entertaining each other with photos of our grandkids!

The Bible tells us to entertain strangers because, who knows, they may be angels! Years ago we entertained Fresh Air Fun children and a foster child—and I tell you, they were *not* angels! But they were adorable and I look back warmly to many fond memories. We also had an exchange student and a variety of European guests related to Hugo's business. Our friends, Amy and Hermie (both now in heaven) were experts at hospitality. They entertained friends (like us!), adopted a child, and foster-parented a good number of teenagers. I always admired their great love of the Lord, and the way they carried it into everything they said and did.

Going forward, I'd like to once again be more hospitable. A couple of Easters ago I felt led to have an Easter buffet for those with nowhere to go on that family-type day. We ended up with just two guests—my good friend, Barbara, from church and a new friend, Betsy, who later attended some of our Bible studies. Someday perhaps I'll have a retreat home in Ocean Grove, NJ, on the Atlantic Ocean—to entertain people, while entertaining God-inspired thoughts.

Entertainment is big business. We never seem to tire of it.
But because it amuses and diverts us, we must be on our guard.
It can waste time, compromise our values, and separate us from God.

I enjoy TV movies, but they'll consume my life if I let them.
I think I sometimes misuse them as an escape or a procrastination.
And so many contain excessive cursing, sex, and violence.

A person's character is evident by the entertainment he/she chooses.
Our time is limited and precious—so I will seek, not so much to
be entertained, as to entertain (spoken in true St. Francis fashion)!

What About You?

1. Have you read or heard the Prayer of St. Francis? If not, try "Googling' it.

2. What conclusions do you come to as your carefully consider *your* favorite types of entertainment?

3. In a very real way, we *are* the thoughts we entertain. What thoughts have *you* been entertaining lately?

Marvel

July 1, 2010

We take too much for granted and don't marvel enough at the amazing life we're living. Just being alive, able to think and love and make decisions... All is a marvelous mystery! The more we learn about nature the more we can marvel at the Hand that designed it. And the more we learn about ourselves the more we realize what a "piece of work" we truly are!

I'm so glad I learned Psalm 139 by heart. I often repeat the line that says, *Your works are wonderful! I know that full well.* The Psalms overflow with praise and awe for a God that can do anything! One of my favorite songs is "How Great Thou Art," by Stuart Hine, who lived to age 100. His words express the reverence and amazement that comes upon us when we take time to marvel:

> *...when I in awesome wonder, consider all the worlds thy hands have made. I see the stars; I hear the rolling thunder. Thy power throughout the universe displayed.*

Today, it's easier than ever to wrap our minds around the unexpected, the extraordinary, and the "impossible." Movies like "Avatar" stretch our thinking, so God's promise of a new heaven and a new earth (with marvelous things we can't begin to describe or even imagine) seems well within the realm of possibility. Someday God will amaze us in a grandiose way. Meanwhile he's given us plenty in the here and now to marvel at. I marvel at the moon against the daytime sky, the way our neighbor's dog can walk using only his front legs (thanks to a special set of wheels for his hind legs), and the way I can "Google" important information in a matter of seconds.

*I marvel at how God responds to my deepest concerns, gets me through
the rough spots, and arranges wonderful "coincidences"—like my
hearing "How Great Thou Art" sung twice today!*

*I marvel at baby Jessica—coming into our world at just the right time.
God answered so many of our prayers with that one special miracle.
May she and I share the greatest of joys--loving the Lord.*

*I marvel at human ingenuity: electricity, cars, airplanes, computers…
yet there's more hate than ever. How passionately we long for the day
when we'll marvel at how it all works out to your glory, dear Lord.*

What About You?

1. Another of my favorite songs is "The Wonder of It All." What songs help *you* to marvel at miracles (both little and big) in the past, present and future?

2. What Psalm(s) come closest to expressing the way *you* feel?

3. What are some things that fill you with awe and amazement?

Open

July 4, 2010

Open my eyes, that I may see glimpses of truth Thou hast for me;
Place in my hands the wonderful key that shall unclasp and set me free.
Refrain:
Silently now I wait for thee, ready my God, Thy will to see,
Open my eyes, illumine me, Spirit divine!
Open my ears, that I may hear voices of truth thou sendest clear;
And while the wave notes fall on my ear, everything false will disappear.
Open my mouth, and let me bear, gladly the warm truth everywhere;
Open my heart and let me prepare love with Thy children thus to share.

This old favorite, written in 1895 by Clara H. Scott comes right to mind when I ponder the word *open*. And now, thanks to my friend, "Google," I can have it playing in the background as I write this. It talks about opening our eyes, ears, mouth and heart to learning and growing in God's direction, so we can sidestep the false as we follow God's will for our lives.

I always wanted to start a non-profit to officially help people, so when Mom died I followed that "pull" on my life—and have found great joy in doing so. God prepared me for it by giving me the opportunity to learn how to handle financials while working in Hugo's international marketing firm. I called our foundation *Open Doors, an Amazing Grace Foundation* in honor and memory of my mom, Grace. We've been helping people for more than ten years now, and I've learned so much by experiencing both success and failure along the way.

Open my heart and mind, Lord, to a bigger vision of our future together.
Proverbs 10 reminds me that there's wisdom and a fountain of life
in words spoken—but violence and ruin in too many foolish words.

I claim the "choice silver" tongue that nourishes many, as described in Proverbs.
I open my ears to listen better when others speak or you call my name.
I open my heart to see, feel and address the needs of others.

I open my home to all kinds of people, for activities that honor you.
Good things happen whenever I move ahead on a prompt or premonition.
I go confidently through whatever doors you open for me.

What About You?

1. What "doors" has God opened for *you*?

2. How have *you* opened up new possibilities and new avenues of hope for others? How have others done that for you?

3. How can we develop a closer relationship with God so he'll be very much with us as we encounter changes and open new "chapters" in our lives?

Produce

July 5, 2010

It's certainly fun (for a while anyway) to sit around and relax. But, even in retirement—perhaps even *more* in retirement, when we can focus on our talents/interests and God's commands—we're called to be productive. In Matthew 7:15-20 Jesus says that actions tell the story: *A good tree produces good fruit; a bad tree produces bad fruit.* And the Book of James stresses "works" in tandem with faith—because faith alone doesn't cut it.

Yesterday Hugo and I took the Sabbath for its intended purpose: to do God-related things (like watching Joel Osteen on TV, attending church) and refreshing, recreational things—like going for a nice evening walk, reading, thinking of others in active ways. And of course, we did patriotic things for Fourth of July—like saying a special prayer for our country and watching the "Capitol Fourth" program televised from Washington, DC. We left the parades and fireworks to the younger crowd, especially in this unusually hot, 90 degree heat.

Today, the "day off" connected with Independence Day, we decided to *produce.* I worked diligently on a new Web site for our big Dogfest event in August. Thankfully, I'm a fast writer since it's my favorite way of producing, so I was able to get all the content to the person helping me. Now I'm ready to do more of the challenging and rewarding activities on my "to-do" list. I'm blessed with so many great "things to do" that I tend to feel overwhelmed, and things *do* suffer—like Jessie's "Woof a Week" newsletter, which seems to have dwindled to every 2 or 3 weeks. But, with God's help, I know I can keep producing in the direction he guides me.

As humans we produce both good and bad fruit. I'm so glad Christianity stresses forgiveness, which gives us fresh new starts, deserved or not. It gives us courage to try new things and, if need be, to try again.

Two women in the lineage of Jesus are non-Jews known for their fruit: Ruth, who followed her Jewish mother-in-law and served the Lord, and Rahab, who hid Joshua's spies and saved their lives and hers.

In the New Testament a Roman Centurion (Acts 10) also bore good fruit. God used him to show Peter that Christianity is for all people. Let's look for and produce as much good fruit as we can each day!

What About You?

1. By age 13, Jesus was already "about his Father's business" (Luke 2:41-52). How are *you* "about your Father's business?"

2. What do you consider to be some of the best things ever produced? Why?

3. What types of "things" should we be striving to produce during our time here on earth?

Credit

July 6, 2010

"Give credit where credit is due," they say. (Hope they pay it back when the bill comes!) We live in a credit-crazy world, where we buy things before we pay for them and vie to take as much credit as we can for ourselves—both money-wise and glory-wise. I need to attend to both types in my everyday life. I definitely have to be more cautious in extracting credit from banks. Even now, the line of credit on our house keeps growing as we spend more than we take in each month. We'll address that tomorrow with our new estate planner.

Awhile back I read Dale Carnegie's classic, *How to Win Friends and Influence People*, and something it contained about the glory-type credit has stayed with me all these years. Carnegie suggests that, whenever possible, we give others (or let them take) credit—even if it's not totally due to them. I think of this often when people tell me something or make a helpful suggestion. My first tendency is to quickly say that I already thought of or tried that, rather than graciously saying "A good idea! Thanks!"

We don't have to always be right, or get the upper hand, or take over a conversation or situation. There's more satisfaction in sitting back and letting others feel good about themselves. It takes nothing from us to refrain from stating the obvious when it brings unnecessary attention to the "elephant in the room"—or to encourage someone by giving them credit even if it isn't totally due to them. The rewards of this approach far exceed any credit we can grab for ourselves.

I wish I were better at following this sage advice. At least I keep
it in mind, and I'm far better off for that. Sometimes I do it right—and
each time I do, it paves the way for doing it right the next time.

Help me, Lord, to be generous in giving and sharing the credit.
Help me to be sincere and empowering—and not an attention seeker.
Let me especially credit those closest to me, who need it most.

The song "Just a Closer Walk with Thee" has a line that says:
Credit (or Grant it) Jesus is my plea. I prefer "credit" as a reminder
that the One who deserves all the credit and glory is you, Lord.

What About You?

1. What credit-giving or credit-taking examples have *you* experienced?

2. What people, past or present, deserve the most credit?

3. How should we react when people credit us for something, either deserved or not deserved?

Play

"All work and no play makes Jack a dull boy," says the old adage. And I was able to Google up a couple more sayings that go *way* back:

> *It is better to play than do nothing.*
> (Confucious, Chinese teacher/philosopher, 551-479 BC)

> *You can discover more about a person in an hour of play*
> *than a year of conversation.*
> (Plato, ancient Greek philosopher, 428-348 BC)

Jesus came to bring us abundant life, and to my way of thinking, that includes a fair dose of fun and games. I don't mean parent-directed sports and structured activities that add stress to our schedules while draining our financial resources. I mean taking delight in everyday things following the example of the late Leo Buscaglia (author, speaker, hugger, and proponent of agape love), who said: "I get wildly enthusiastic about little things...I play with leaves. I skip down the street and run against the wind."

This past week my dog, Jessie, and I visited our friends in the Memory Care (Alzheimer's) wing of a nearby facility. I answer a lot of the same questions each time we go, but we always have a great time. During this particular visit we came prepared with some fun and games like learning each others' names (Fortunately there were five Marys!) and sharing what we know by heart: songs, nursery rhymes, jumprope ditties, etc. We ended by pooling our knowledge about history, medicine, entertainment, and the world. I kissed each one goodbye for the first time since we've been going. Why? Because it seemed natural—we were now happier and closer to each other because we had "played" together.

*The playful Jesus attended weddings and banquets, and bantered
with a Greek woman before healing her daughter long-distance.
He also promised life abundant to those who follow Him.*

*Help me, dear Lord, to find child-like joy in wholesome fun and games.
Let me spread good cheer and lift others' spirits
while not minimizing their challenges and heartaches.*

*Let me take time each day to play a bit at what I enjoy most
and laugh at myself as I flounder doing something brand new...
and see your sense of humor all around me!*

What About You?

1. Some people say that God had a sense of humor when He made a camel, an otter, or when... How might you complete that sentence, using your own experience and opinions?

2. When has lightening up and seeing the humor in a situation worked to your advantage? What sort of difference did it make?

3. How can an element of playfulness enrich our relationships with God and others?

Heed

July 10, 2010

Webster's New World Dictionary defines *heed* as "paying close attention" to something. In my case, I believe this word especially relates to my sensing, and acting upon, God's subtle (and sometimes not-so-subtle) "nudges." I followed a nudge when I had my first at-home Bible Study, the first of several. I also paid attention to God's nudge to find and adopt our dog Jessie, and found that it led to all kinds of wonderful new friends and experiences.

It's often a challenge to distinguish God's "still small voice" from our own thoughts and desires. God gave me a few warnings regarding our investment in a Las Vegas hotel condo—I sure wish I'd heeded them instead following my own agenda. My impetuosity also got us into trouble years before that, when I was too quick to rent office space before we actually needed it and ended up having to keep the empty offices for a full year without ever using them. I also gave and loaned money to people too hastily and sorely regretted it.

Sometimes God's nudges are incredible blessings—like the morning about 12 years ago when I awoke very early, literally singing a new song. I jumped right up and wrote down a chorus and five verses effortlessly—heeding a call and capturing a once-in-a-lifetime gift I didn't ask for or expect. I then sang the song into a tape recorder to preserve the tune. We've sung it in church and at a retreat and on several other occasions. I'm so glad I heeded God's prompt. In fact, it's been the joy of my life to follow through on what I feel called to do, no matter how tedious or challenging it may become. That includes finishing this word-a-day compendium, and using it to draw myself and others closer to the Lord.

Just this morning God sent another "special delivery" nudge my way.
Book Launch ideas came fast and furiously, as Hugo walked the dog.
Now I'm all set to work on that big project the day after tomorrow.

Tomorrow is the Sabbath. Per our new set-up I'll devote it to the Lord.
It's no accident that these ideas came on a Saturday, so Sunday's free.
It always works out better when we heed his commandments.

We heed the examples and instructions in his Holy Word—for our own good.
When we acknowledge God, he directs our paths. When we treat others
well, forgive often, refuse to worry, etc. a joyful peace is ours!

What About You?

1. When have you been nudged by God's Spirit or Word? When did you heed well and when did you not?

2. What Biblical examples come to mind when we think of heeding and not heeding?

3. Dad's advice to arrive at the workplace early served me well. What well-heeded human advice and/or God-given prompts have made the biggest difference in your life?

Humble

This is being written on the following day—no work on Sundays, remember! I almost forgot this. Actually, I didn't forget; I just tried to ignore it long enough to make some corrections on our Dogfest Web site. As Hugo was calling me to hurry to the living room so I wouldn't miss Joel Osteen's joke of the week, I was chugging along nicely on my editing. But suddenly, a minute before Joel's joke, my computer absolutely refused to let me do *anything*! Sometimes, when we don't humble ourselves as we should, *God* humbles us!

The funny thing is…I knew the word *humble* was ear-marked for this day by the time I opened the refrigerator to search out something for breakfast. I forget why I felt the need to humble myself on this particular day, but this aptly timed computer glitch has indeed left me duly humbled. And, can you believe… just the day before this, God had warned me *not* to try and steal his day for my own purposes. See how stubborn we humans are! Especially me.

Humility is something I've been seeking for a long time. I recall going to a church retreat more than a decade ago and telling my small discussion group that my goal in coming was to become more humble. One woman looked surprised, which I took as a compliment. Maybe she didn't see as much brashness and attention-seeking in me as I did. I certainly have always flourished on the praise of others, something I've tried for years to eradicate (or at least lessen). The silent times and the contemplative nature of the retreat activities were just the tools I needed to help me see things more clearly and draw closer to my *humble* goal.

Pastor Chuck's sermon yesterday was about Psalm 73--when life is
unfair. The psalmist complains about the wicked thriving and the good
suffering. Then he goes into the temple...and his perspective changes.

He tells God how he feels, recalling that God has guided him in the past.
He declares that God is holding him and will welcome him into glory.
We, too, can go to God during our darkest times and be empowered.

Jesus says to take the worst seat (Lk 14:10) and be humble like a child
because the meek will inherit the earth and surpass the haughty.
Help us, Lord, to think and act more humbly.

What About You?

1. Who do you think exemplifies a truly humble spirit -- one that isn't solely motivated by present or future rewards?

2. When have you seen or experienced the results of haughtiness and/or humility in yourself or in others?

3. In church I thought of Mary and Martha—and I see myself as Martha when Jesus says: Martha, *Martha (Ruth, Ruth), you are worried and upset about so many things. Mary has chosen what is best, and it will not be taken away from her. (Luke 10:38-42)* How can we, like Mary, let go of our concerns and sit spellbound at feet of the Master?

167

Supersede

July 16, 2010

Our interim pastor, Harold Smith, would often change his sermon at the last minute because of what he termed "new marching orders from the Boss." When we'd open the bulletin on Sunday morning we'd wonder (and rightfully so) whether the sermon message would stand, or if it would be superseded by a new one, fresh from the Spirit of God. We all enjoyed Pastor Harold's openness and flexibility, and because if it, we're now more attuned to listening, following, and letting God supersede in our lives, too!

I'm known for making *too* many changes, replacing *this* with *that* until I drive people crazy. That, I'm sure, is not what God has in mind with our Word of the Day. Perhaps he wants me to do less changing and controlling, and let him do the changing and controlling. I tend to be like those editors who say they never finish, they just run out of time. I need to keep in mind quotes like "Leave well enough alone" and my favorite Shakespearean one: "Striving to better oft we mar what is well." And the one I really need: "Let go, and let God (take over.)"

Matthew, chapter 5, is filled with Jesus using his authority to change things around—and his commands *always* supersede the former ones. He expands "Thou shalt not kill" to include being angry with someone without cause and calling someone names. He expands adultery to include looking lustfully at someone. And he supercedes oath-taking with a "yes" or "no"—and an "eye for an eye" with a turning of the other cheek. Hardest of all is his replacing *hate* your enemy with *love* your enemy.

168

Make me responsive to your guidance, Lord--like Pastor Harold is.
May Jesus' teachings override my selfish agenda and lavish lifestyle.
Through your Spirit I can get a glimpse of what is higher and better.

Some of the best Scriptures talk about new things superseding the old:
In 2 Co 5:17 Paul says that everything is new when we're "in Christ."
Rev 21:1 describes a new heaven and earth to replace former ones...

When this happens our tears will be wiped away (Rev 21:4). Pain and
death will be no more. Instead, marvelous mysteries will be revealed.
And it will be truly awesome because Jesus' love supersedes all!

What About You?

1. What needs to be superseded (changed, replaced, done away with) in *your* life? In our world?

2. How can we team up with God to make those adjustments?

3. What are some examples of superseding being successful—and superseding not being so successful?

Enlarge

July 21, 2010

Think big!! OK!!! Like Jabez did. He is mentioned in just one verse of the Bible (1 Chronicles 4:10), yet his short prayer is pondered and prayed by millions—thanks to Bruce Wilkinson's book, "The Prayer of Jabez." To refresh our memories, this is his prayer:

Oh, that You would bless me indeed, and enlarge my territory, that Your hand would be with me, and that You would keep me from evil, that I may not cause pain.

It's certainly a noble prayer, undeniably self-centered yet filled with caring for others and faith in an all-powerful God.

This is an appropriate word for us today because Hugo and I are in the process of enlarging our boundaries by moving ahead in new directions. This afternoon we met with our estate planner, Sidney, who is now instrumental in helping us to clarify our goals and pursue our dreams. He and his assistant Leah helped us to make some financial changes that will carry us through our remaining years without depleting our entire estate. This is exciting! He's already found ways to lessen our spending and stretch our assets.

Pruning out what holds us back is the hardest part of enlarging. We'll be saying goodbye to some well-liked service providers who, for one reason or another, need to be phased out. I sense some big changes ahead as we hone in on new and exciting ways to use this final chapter of our earthly lives. We're grateful to those who have helped us in the past, but now we'll have a new team to get us successfully, and literally, from here to eternity!

Larger isn't always better. Look what God told Gideon to do (Jg 7:1-8).
Yet God told Abram to scan the sky and imagine a day when his
descendants would outnumber the stars overhead.

Paul was content with either want or abundance (Phil 4:11-13).
Like Paul, we can be satisfied in our present state while simultaneously
struggling toward God's upward call in Christ Jesus (Phil 3:12-14).

Lord, enlarge me in ways that magnify you: my vision, outreach, caring...
Prune out what's stale, useless, draining, or just plain rotten.
Grant me here-and-now contentment as I grow in your direction.

What About You?

1. What needs enlarging or pruning in *your* life? How can that be accomplished?

2. Sometimes we enlarge the negative, letting it frighten or immobilize us. How can we effectively ward off and/or deal with that kind of enlarging?

3. What are some examples of "less is more?" What should only be enlarged under certain circumstances? What should we be constantly enlarging?

Measure

The Psalmist (39:4) asks God to help him know the measure of his days so he can appreciate how fleeting his life is—and use the time allotted to him in the best possible ways. It's good for us to also be reminded that *today* is all we have to work with now, and we should make the most of it.

Ours is a God of exact measurements, isn't he? He provided food (manna) for the traveling Israelites and told them exactly how much to harvest each day—just what they needed for that day. Only on the day before the Sabbath could they take extra for the following day-of-rest. They soon learned that a modest amount supplied their daily needs, and an excessive amount spoiled and was unusable. Maybe we can take a lesson from this... that we, too, should conserve, do with less, and measure our success and happiness in ways other than material possessions.

God also demands honesty and equality in our measuring systems— "a full and just measure" (Deuteronomy 25:15), he says, "will prolong our days." He requires a genuineness that doesn't change according to circumstances. ("not two kinds of measures, large and small"). Take, for example, James' warning not to treat rich people differently from poor people (2:1-5).

The best "measure" for our lives is Jesus. When in doubt, we can ask ourselves "What would Jesus do?" He gives us the very best standard and example. He doesn't just say, "Love others"—he says, "Love others as I have loved you."

Measurements like hours and days give us the secure boundaries we need.
What if the roads had no centerline, or the cars had no speedometers?
What if we had no numbers on which to base our plans and decisions?

What if Jesus hadn't come to set our hearts toward eternity?
Thankfully, we have the measures and means to prolong/enrich our days.
We have you, dear Father, Son, and Holy Spirit.

Jesus said: The measure you give will be the measure you get (Mt 7:2).
So, let's give him our all—and, in return, we'll find our lives
filled and overflowing with blessings galore!

What About You?

1. How do you measure success/happiness/God's approval?

2. The handwriting on the wall (Daniel 5) warned King Belshazzar that his days as king were numbered because he wasn't measuring up. In what ways are we as individuals and communities not measuring up today? What can we do about it?

3. Do you believe that when it's your turn to step onto God's scales, Jesus will step on with you so it balances perfectly? If so, how does that belief influence the way you live today?

Receive

July 25, 2010

The quote Paul attributes to Christ in Acts 20:35 (*It's better to give than to receive.*) is so much a part of our Christian outlook that we often forget that we are also called to receive. Just as Moses received the Ten Commandments, David received God's forgiveness, and the sick people received their miracles, so we can have the honor of receiving God's priceless gifts—things like his Word, his Spirit, his blessing and favor.

Pastor Chuck closes our weekly worship services by reminding us that it's not by trying to make up for the past or by making great promises for the future, but it's by receiving God's grace that we find the peace and the power to live each day to the fullest.

The disciples hovered together in a locked room after Mary Magdalene told them that she had seen and even spoken with the risen Christ. They were nervous (actually scared to death), yet they were expectant, wondering what was going to happen. Then suddenly Jesus was among them, greeting them with a loving *shalom*. How boundless their joy must have been (expressed in the CEV as *They became very happy*.)

Jesus' next words were words of commission: *I am sending you, just as the Father has sent me*. Then he did something truly miraculous: he breathed on them and said, *Receive the Holy Spirit*. And the world has never been the same. (See Jn 20:19-23.)

In order to give, we first receive; we can't give what we don't have.
With great gifts, like the Spirit, come great commissions.
We needn't be fearful or hesitant: With God all things are possible!

Let's graciously receive well-deserved compliments,
guidance from wiser, more experienced people—and even
admonishment and criticism that lifts us to higher ground.

Jas 1:17 says "All good things come from the Father," so we must remember
to give thanks and glory to the One who gives and sustains our lives...
then pass on as much good as we can, as often as we can.

What About You?

1. In what ways is it better to give than receive?

2. How can being gracious receivers make us more gracious givers?

3. Who are the most giving people you know (have known, or know of)?
    What can we learn from them? Who stands out as a receiver, and what
    can we learn from *that* person?

Relish

July 29, 2010

I'm not one to put relish on my burgers and franks, and the more I ponder this interesting word the more I realize that I'm also not taking time to relish my many blessings. I'm too busy feeling anxious and rushing around to meet some self-imposed deadline—or thinking up new ideas that will involve more of the same.

Fortunately I enjoy (to a large degree) creating new projects and "biting off more than I can chew." But I must admit that it can get out of control. Today's word is a good reminder to slow down and relish the goodness, the beauty, and the love that surround me. One of my favorite stage shows is "Our Town," because it's a stark reminder that we all tend to take the most important and precious things (and people) for granted.

I'm making an effort to enjoy this lovely time of year despite my over-zealous schedule. It's been extremely hot so far this summer, but I'm making time to relax on our covered patio with cat in lap and dog at feet. I enjoy the view and the breeze as I relish things like:

* just being alive,

* chatting with a God who has an awful lot to teach me, and

* having inspiring missions and people in my life.

This type of relish provides the "oil" that keeps our "gears" running smoothly so we don't burn ourselves out or lose sight of the priceless gifts right in our own backyards. It adds true flavor and spice to our lives.

Today I learned that a church in Florida is using my booklet "Following Jesus"
in its prison ministry—with great enthusiasm and great success.
Such good news deserves a little relishing!

Also today, Hugo and I relished seeing friends we hadn't seen in ages.
It was a fantastic side trip from our routine, self-appointed tasks.
We were inspired by the way they help others and enjoy their leisure.

This is the Day the Lord has made—let's rejoice and be glad in it. (Ps 118:24)
Let's relish all that's good, helpful, encouraging and hopeful…
so we're better equipped to use time and talents in God-ordained ways.

What About You?

1. What keeps you from relishing your blessings as much as you should? How can you change that?

2. I exercise often because I relish energy and good health. What do your top priorities reveal about you?

3. Most of all, I relish my relationship with the Lord. How can I (and you) draw closer to God on an ongoing basis?

Unite

July 30, 2010

Here's an upbeat word for an upbeat day. The weather is ideal—sunny and brisk in the morning, working its way to a bearable summer temperature. "This is exactly the weather I want for our outdoor Dogfest next month," I boldly told God. Hugo reminded me that I'll take what we get, and I reminded him that it doesn't hurt to ask and let God know the desires of our hearts. I was glad Hugo didn't further remind me that we're holding this on a Sunday afternoon and with so much to do I'll have to miss church that day. (I would have countered, "But I'll be sure to watch Joel Osteen on TV!")

Two Dogfest "angels" (volunteers for the event) answered my frantic request for help with the overall planning. I'm good at thinking up ideas and envisioning the end product, but I'm not good at getting from here to there. I don't delegate well and then go crazy trying to manage all the logistics. I asked Pat and Julie, two creative and well-organized animal lovers, to be my "inner circle." I know that more will get accomplished with them than with many angels looking to me for direction.

Julie and Pat were asked and both came. You might say that we united with one purpose in mind—to make this major event happen with as few glitches as possible. We even tried setting up one of the three gazebos we'll be using at the event and it looks great! Now the ball's in my court, so to speak, until I get the necessary email addresses to Julie, who will be in charge of matching our large group of volunteers with the many jobs to be done that day. Whew, it sure feels good to unite with others and not try to handle everything myself.

Where one or two are gathered in his name, Jesus is there. (Mt 18:20)
When two agree and pray in unison (18:19), God acts on it.
In 1 Peter 4:8 it says that being united in love should top the list.

Lessons from the fables of Aesop (a Greek slave, 620-560 BC) include:
"United we stand, divided we fall" and "Unity gives strength." His story,
"Bundle of Sticks," tells why a father wants his sons to stick together.

Our dog Jessie has to work on her relationship with two neighborhood dogs.
Carl of "Carl's Calm Canines" will be the qualified peacemaker.
We're expecting Jessie to become a good example of "United we stand!"

What About You?

1. What are some examples of unity in action?

2. In what very specific ways can the word "unite" inspire meaningful
    action in *your* life?

3. What do you think of the words to "They'll Know We are Christians by
    Our Love" (after Googling the lyrics or locating it in a songbook)? How
    do they inspire you?

Wash

July 31, 2010

Today's word inspired me to finally give our dog Jessie a hosing down and soaping up. It was a lovely sunny, summer day so washing her was a joy for both of us. And she looked fresh and shiny for a special barbeque she, Hugo and I attended today. It was held at the Memory Care Center (Alzheimer's wing) in a nearby extended-care facility that Jessie and I visit regularly. Everybody loved Jessie and she loved the hotdogs and hamburgers! They had a great musician and singer entertaining with his keyboard. Maybe we can "book" him for some of our charitable events… maybe even Dogfest.

It was indeed a washy day for me because I also did our usual loads of sheets, towels and clothing. And, since I washed Jessie, I also washed her towels, her car-seat cover and her fleece-lined seatbelt harness. I really washed up a storm, didn't I? But when I think about it, I realize that we can wash the dirt off our bodies and our accessories, but we can't wash the stains from our hearts and souls. Only Jesus can cleanse us so we sparkle like new inside and out, because (as the Gospel songs say) *Jesus washes our sins away!* His death on the cross leaves us looking good.

Pilate tried to wash his hands of Jesus, and sometimes we do, too. But we can't wash Jesus away once we have contact with him, and our efforts to do so only *keep* him away. We, like Pilate, are pressured by others to do away with Jesus—in our case, to keep his name out of public prayers so we won't offend anyone or drive a wedge between those who worship him and those who don't. But Jesus says: *Don't be ashamed of me or I'll be ashamed of you when I come into my glory with the Father and the Holy Angels. (Mk 8:38, Lk 9:26)*

Jerry and Larraine help African families get clean water and schools.
Joanne and Kevin visit Guatemala each summer to spread the Gospel.
They all help to wash away problems and change lives for the better.

Jesus praised the woman who washed his feet with her tears (Lk 7:44).
He washed the feet of his disciples (Jn 13:4-17), and then
instructed them to follow his example and do likewise for each other.

Jesus chided those who used "clean" cups and dishes in line with holy
guidelines, yet were filled with greed and selfishness. (Mt 23:24-26)
First clean the inside, he said, then the outside will be clean, too.

What About You?

1. How can we express our adoration for Jesus in ways that are just as heartfelt as washing his feet with tears?

2. In what ways, small and large, do we wash our hands of Jesus and/or let greed and selfishness into our lives? What can we do about that?

3. What do you think I mean by saying that we can't wash Jesus away--and trying to do so only *keeps* him away?

Delegate

August 1, 2010

Today is Sunday, a day to relax, refresh, and reflect. I might jot down things to help me going forward, but I don't work on them yet--since the Sabbath is a day set apart from the rest of the week, as God intended it to be. While walking Jessie before church a beautiful melody came to mind, something simple that I played on the piano years ago. It's an ideal piece to play on my "new" keyboard that a church friend recently gave me, so I enlarged the music to it (accommodating the change in my eyesight) and now I'm all set to start filling our living area with beautiful thoughts, words, and melodies.

Amid all these lovely non-work activities the word *delegate* has crept in to remind me that I have to stop spending so much time and energy working on or thinking about my two big projects. Other things are just as important—and maybe even more important! I must learn to let go of many of the details and responsibilities by delegating them to trustworthy people. Today Joel Osteen (TV preacher) talked about Jesus' "inner circle" of three. Just Peter, James, and John joined him as he raised a child from death, spoke with Moses and Elijah on the mountain top, and prayed in the garden before he was crucified (Mk 5:37-43; 9:2-13; and 14:32-42). As the ones closest to Jesus, they were especially delegated to spread the Word.

At church this morning Pastor Chuck told a fictional story about Jesus returning to heaven after his Ascension and telling the heavenly host about his experience on earth. One archangel asked what would happen if those he delegated to spread the Good News failed to do it.

182

*Jesus' answer was "I have no other plan." The disciples rose to the task
and here we are today, a living testament to the great job they did.
Now it's our turn to run with the task and spread the Word.*

*I'm honored to be your delegate, Lord Jesus. You're ever in my thoughts.
With your help, I'll see things from a higher, more loving perspective.
I'll be a channel that connects heaven and earth in my own unique way.*

*In order to be a good delegate I must be willing to delegate to others.
I'll eliminate whatever holds me back or leads me in the wrong direction.
I'll entrust my time, talent, and treasures to your guidance and care.*

What About You?

1. What are you now doing that would be better delegated to someone else?

2. What sort of responsibilities has Jesus delegated to us?

3. Who is, or should be, in your inner circle—to help you view things from a higher perspective, focus on your mission in life, and eliminate or delegate wisely?

Nurture

What a wonderful word *nurture* is! All three meanings conjure up warm, fuzzy feelings. The first meaning is to give tender care that helps something or someone to grow and develop. The second meaning is to give encouragement so the person or thing can thrive and be successful. The third meaning is to keep something in mind for a long time, allowing it to grow and deepen.

When I think back over my life I realize how powerful early nurturing is. I got special nurturing from my maternal grandmother who gave me extra attention because I was a third, unexpected child born 22 months after my sister. She wanted to be sure I would grow and develop properly. My mom told me that Grandma would hold my hand and sing me to sleep. I'm also told that I was the easiest, happiest of the babies—until Grandma died when I was two years old. Then I became moody and cranky.

My maternal grandfather lived another year or two. I remember him telling the three of us kids great stories that always ended with a monkey stepping on a piece of tin and Grandpa saying "The tin bended and the story ended!" I had a short time with my grandparents, but their loving nurture helped me to grow into a confident adult who loves holding hands, singing, and story-telling. For 17 years I led the children's choir at church. In my mid-fifties I was drawn to Biblical storytelling—learning Scripture and telling it in my own heartfelt way. I learned the entire Book of Mark in just three months--then Jonah, the Love Chapter, Psalm 139, and the Book of James. I'm sure my grandparents are looking down with pride and joy as I look up to them in gratitude.

My therapy dog Jessie and I visited friends in a nursing home today.
The funny thing is, we get (as well as give) nurturing whenever we visit.
Proverbs 11:25 says that one who waters is him/herself watered.

The keyboard a friend gave me is bringing me closer to the Lord.
It's in a very visible location so I see it often throughout the day.
It beckons me to take a break and learn an inspirational piece.

God has sent caring, faithful people to nurture me in so many ways.
He's carried me through tough times and put dreams in my heart.
I, in turn, strive to nurture and encourage others—with his help.

What About You?

1. Inspirational music, Holy Scriptures, and kindness from others surely nurture *my* soul. What nurtures *yours*?

2. Who has nurtured you? Who have you nurtured?

3. What are some things that have happened or come to be because someone (perhaps even you) nurtured some thought or possibility?

Motivate

August 9, 2010

We can all use a little extra motivation—to speed up, slow down, work harder, take it easier, think of others more, think of ourselves more... As our lives zig-zag in all these (and countless other) directions, it helps to have an overall goal, motto and/or mission for our lives—to keep the big picture and the major destination in mind. It's like a farmer with a hand plow, focusing on a distant object in order plow a straight line.

When our friend Lois recently visited, we talked about the pictures I put in my see-through mouse pad years ago. The one of the bride and groom has led to our daughter and Danny, and a marvelous added joy— our granddaughter, Jessica. The picture relating to the Kids'n'Kritters project no doubt motivated the adoption of our dog, Jessie. And along with Jessie has come a myriad of blessings—through her therapy work, her book, and the big fundraising events, like Dogfest. The two remaining pictures are simmering, waiting to become an actual retreat house in Ocean Grove for our non-profit foundation and condo in Sanibel, Florida, for us.

Lois said that many years ago she wrote down what she wanted in life: a wonderful husband, and of course children. She put the paper in her Bible and forgot about it. Years later she found it again. By then she was married to the man of her dreams—who had two children, so she became an instant mother. In addition, she and Don had a child together, Klara, and adopted a baby in need of a good home—Ben. We both agreed that we have received over and above what we ever imagined. That's how God generally works, when we dare to believe and dream big.

*Motivation makes a huge difference! I'm basically shy, but when
I'm impassioned I have no fear, just courage and enthusiasm!
Norman Vincent Peale and others have similar stories.*

*Thanks, Lord, for sparking interests and working miracles in my life.
How can I motivate others to look to you for those things, too?
I'd like to do it through my writing and personal interactions.*

*Help me see things in perspective and not do more harm than good.
May my greatest passion always be for you, Lord,
and a life well lived for your glory. Amen.*

What About You?

1. What most motivates you to work harder? to make changes? to draw closer to God?

2. When have others motivated you (and vice versa)?

3. What life's goal, motto, or mission would best keep your life on track?

Raise

August 10, 2010

Right this moment I *raise* my hands heavenward and say, "Thank you, Lord!" for so much: for sending Julie today to help things along with the Dogfest, for people responding positively to both of my big projects, for a husband who is so loving and supportive, for the dog who lies on the floor beside me as I work on the computer, for an adorable granddaughter and a wonderful daughter who's doing a great job mothering her, for Danny who loves and spoils them both, for a Savior who makes life worth living no matter what... and that's just the beginning!

I also *raise* my hand and say, "Here am I, Lord, send me!" There's a lot to be done and, with your help, I can make a difference. The more I move ahead and do what I can (as best I can) for your sake and for others, the more you pave the way with favor and delightful miracles. And when things don't always fall the way I want them to, I know you're with me to comfort me, guide me, and call me to task again and again. Every day is a learning experience, and I volunteer to keep growing in your direction, Lord, wherever it may take me.

May I *raise* a question or two, Lord? Why me? Why am I so blessed? I can't help but think of that wonderful song Elvis sang called "Who am I?" (by Rusty Goodman):

> When I think of how He came so far from glory,
> Came to dwell among the lowly such as I...
> To suffer shame and such disgrace on Mount Calvary take my place
> Then I ask myself this question, Who am I?

>> Who am I that the King would bleed and die for?
>> Who am I that He would pray "Not my will—thine, Lord?"
>> The answer I may never know why He ever loved me so,
>> that to an old rugged cross He'd go for Who am I?

Jesus was raised up on a cross and suffered agony and humiliation for us.
Then he was raised from the dead and met with believers for forty days.
He then raised his hand and commissioned his followers to go and tell.

I was raised in a Christian home, following generations of believers.
The agnostic I married is still an agnostic after 43 years together.
I love and enjoy him, and trust the Lord to keep drawing him closer...

We raised our daughter in the church and sent her to Christian schools.
I'm so glad that granddaughter Jessica is now going to church, too.
I raise my voice in praise and thanksgiving to the One I love so much.

What About You?

1. What are you raising in *your* life? What do you wish you were raising?

2. God can raise us up from any pit in which we may find ourselves. What examples come to mind in your life or others' lives?

3. If you could ask God anything, what question would you raise? How do you think he would answer?

Calculate

August 16, 2010

This word makes me think of the program our "Good Book Players" put on a few years ago. We'd already done the book of Jonah—directly from the CEV Bible. We added costumes, scenery, humor, and a variety of musical flourishes. It was a real hit and raised over $1,000 for the county's homeless. Our next undertaking was the story of Noah, as compared to Jonah (called the "Noah-Jonah Connection"). Our pastor at the time felt there were no similarities, but I came up with several as I put together a scene in an old-fashioned Sunday School classroom. Each student had his/her own special characteristics which carried throughout the drama.

Several of us dressed like children—two were really children amid "pretend children" like me. I wore a dark wig, braided like my mom used to do it. I was the math wiz, always *calculatin'*—how many days Noah's boat was afloat and all sorts of other things. I spoke in a hillbilly twang and really got into it. We all had a blast and learned a lot about both of those beloved Biblical stories.

I guess God has some more serious calculatin' in mind for me today. For example, I must ask myself if the projects I'm presently so obsessed with are worth the cost. Am I neglecting my husband, my friends, my God? Am I ruining my health? Am I keeping things in balance and perspective? Am I doing or not doing things that I'll regret later? Am I taking time to relax, meditate, pray, nurture the people I have contact with—and really listen to them without my mind wandering? Am I missing out on going places and doing helpful and fun things because of all I choose to put on my agenda? If I had a week to live, would I do anything differently?

Jesus wants us to calculate the cost of following him (Mt 8:20):
"Foxes have dens; birds have nests; but I have nowhere to lay my head."
He promises us, not a rose garden, but a loving relationship.

Thanks, Lord, for reminding me to calculate the value of my activities.
Just this week we got a pat on our backs (article and photo) for Open
Doors' work with the animal rescue groups—time well spent.

Help me to better hear your voice and follow your lead instead of going
headstrong into things that are attractive but of limited value.
The closer I am to you the better I hear you. Speak as I listen, Lord.

What About You?

1. What calculations are you (or should you be) contemplating right now?

2. In Lk 14:27-3 Jesus gives examples of people making important calculations. When have your calculations been off--or right on? What have you learned in both instances?

3. What are some pros and cons of following Jesus today?

Remove

August 19, 2010

There are lots of things I should remove from my life—material things, activities and especially intangibles like being insensitive or judging people--in my mind, and in the words and actions that follow such thoughts. I'd also like to erase things about myself that annoy others, like talking too much and cutting others off while they're speaking.

Jesus tells an interesting story about our tendency to want to remove a splinter from someone else's eye, when we have a whole beam blocking *our* vision! (found in both Matthew 7 and Luke 6). He then tells us to first remove the haughty judgmental streak from ourselves so we can see things in a more godly perspective. It's so easy to criticize, make fun of, and subtly put down another. I found myself doing that twice during our big Dogfest meeting of the volunteers—this terrible type of thinking just comes natural to us humans, I guess. But recognizing something that needs to be removed is the first, necessary step to removing it.

In the same passage Jesus says that what we mete out to others is what is going to be meted out to us. Just think about it! Imagine being treated the way we've at times treated others? Ouch! That hurts. I've disrespected people, considered some better than others, and expected less from those who needed and deserved better. That's like checking out an imaginary splinter in another's eye -- which merely confirms that there's an obstruction in *my* life that needs removing. When I remove it I'll be able to see not the splinter, but the light of potential in another's eye!

*Right afterwards Jesus says not to give dogs what belongs to God--
and not to throw pearls to pigs, to be trampled underfoot.
Obviously we sometimes have to make a judgment call!*

*Some "splinters" we see are actual "beams" we can do nothing about.
Our "pearls" (faith, time, encouragement, etc.) sometimes have
to be removed from those who aren't gaining from them.*

*Remove all deceit from me, Lord, so I'll be more like Nathanael (Jn 1:45-51).
He may have doubted Jesus: "Can anything good come from Nazareth?"
But Jesus immediately saw Nathanael as a deceit-free disciple.*

What About You?

1. What splinters are you noticing in others' eyes? How can God help us to see more clearly and act in line with his will?

2. What thoughts and examples come to mind when pondering today's word?

3. If you could remove something(s) from your life or the world, what would it/they be? What steps can you take toward doing that?

Enthuse

August 23, 2010

"Enthusiasm makes the difference," says Norman Vincent Peale, in his book by that name. He was certainly full of enthusiasm (which means "God within us") in more ways than one. He was super-shy as a young person but became one of the most amazing public speakers of all time. He'd never use notes; he'd just speak from the heart. And what a storyteller he was! How fortunate we were to have been in his congregation for a couple of years when we lived in NYC in the late 1960s and early 1970s.

Today I was full of enthusiasm for all that's happening as our big Dogfest Fun'raiser quickly approaches. I'm on a constant adrenalin rush, which can't last because it isn't good for me—or others around me. But there's so much to do and enjoy (and worry about) as people contact me to ask questions or to sign up to participate. The newspapers are revved up, too, and even the County Executive's office called to be part of the opening ceremonies.

I think God gave me this word today to remind me that enthusiasm is meant to be shared. I think one of the best gifts we can give a person is to enjoy him or her—to be sincerely enthusiastic about what they do and say, and especially about who they are. The best way to enthuse someone is to be enthusiastic ourselves. It's catching! I taught third grade for nine years, so I know that an average but enthusiastic learner is much preferred over a brilliant student with an attitude. And what a joy it is when an enthusiastic teacher can turn that student with an attitude into an enthusiastic learner!

Paul enthusiastically wrote, "Rejoice in the Lord. Again I say, rejoice!"
The psalmist enthusiastically says "This is the day the Lord has made!"
And Jesus surely beamed as he said "I go to prepare a place for you."

What a difference it makes! Enthusiasm enables me to speak out boldly
and not give up; it lets out the "God in me" that
supersedes the negativity we're confronted with daily.

You're the greatest, Lord! May I never lose my enthusiasm for you.
My family and friends are wonderful, too—I enjoy them so much!
Life is an amazing gift—I'm enthused about it and will use it well.

What About You?

1. When has your enthusiasm bubbled over and "infected" others (and vice versa)?

2. What are you most enthused about now? How can you best spread that enthusiasm?

3. What enthusiastic statements can you make to those you love? To those you have trouble liking? To God?

Stretch

There's good stretching and bad stretching. Good stretching can be the type Hugo suggested to me today. Since I've been spending so much time slumping over my computer, my posture is suffering. I especially notice it whenever I look at photos of me taken from the side. To help and encourage me, Hugo gave me a little section from his ebook related to overcoming fatigue at work. He recommends:
- stretching the neck and holding head high (as if pulled upward by a magnet),
- pulling shoulders back while squeezing shoulder blades together and down,
- sticking chest out and tucking belly in, and
- straightening and stretching the back.

Other good stretches are when our reach exceeds our grasp, when we stretch our imaginations, and when we stretch our dollars so they go farther. Bad stretches would be when we stretch the truth for our own selfish purposes, or when we stretch our necks to hear some juicy gossip.

Now that I'm on the "home stretch" in terms of my life here on earth, I want to stretch out everything: my outreach to others, my time with family and friends, my opportunities to smell the roses and enjoy the wonder of it all. But most of all, I want to stretch toward God in any way I can. This Word-a-Day has been an enjoyably wonderful way to do that. I now find myself setting new goals, like being more positive toward others and myself, toning down my obnoxious ways, and being more open and caring toward others.

The more I stretch toward God the more God responds to my stretch.
James 4:8 says: "Come near to God, and God will come near to you."
Whenever I've reached out to the Lord I've never been disappointed.

I believe that "With God all things are possible." (Mt 19:26) I find it
easy to accept the virgin birth, resurrection, life after death, etc.
It's no stretch for me—I look around and within, and I'm convinced.

Faith is a gift that enables us to use time and energy productively
instead of wasting it by doubting and arguing. And as we read, pray,
learn, work, and move in God's direction, our faith increases!

What About You?

1. I wanted our favorite TV preacher, Joel Osteen, to be part of our upcoming book launch project—a stretch, yes. Successful? Yes! When have you made an "impossible" stretch that succeeded?

2. What goals can you set that are now beyond your reach? (Try writing them down and placing them where you'll see them each day...)

3. Which of God's and/or Jesus' miracles do you find easiest and hardest to believe? Which ones can be explained away and which defy explanation? What "miracles" have you personally experienced?

Remind

August 25, 2010

At 6:15 this morning Jessie and I embarked upon our usual adventure—she happily sniffing away, searching out just the right places to leave her mark, and me thinking about anything and everything. But today something awesome took my breath away! A gorgeous well-rounded moon shone brightly in the early-morning sky. Wow! What a great way to be reminded that we are indeed small and short-lived. The things we fuss over and worry about are minuscule in light of something far bigger that's right in front of our eyes!

The wonderful Web site I use to navigate the Scriptures, www.Search-GodsWord.org, led me to a powerful part of Luke's Gospel: 12:22-40. It reminds us that we shouldn't even be concerned about big things, like what we'll eat, drink, or wear. God knows what we need and, if we put him first in our lives, he will take good care of us. In this passage Jesus tells his disciples to sell what they have, give away the proceeds, and build up treasures in heaven. Then he promises that those who are alert and ready to greet him upon his return will get to sit down and be served by *him*!

There are now just a few days until Dogfest, our big charitable event which has grown huge this year. Things can get pretty hectic because so many small details can morph into big problems if unattended. I feel like Lucy in that hysterically funny "I Love Lucy" scene where she tries to keep up with the conveyor belt of candy she's packaging. But no matter what she does, it gets away from her.

Hopefully my conveyor belt of tasks will slow down, not speed up.
I keep thinking about doing less, but I feel God wants me to do more.
Even some of the t-shirts donated to our event say to "Do More!"

I'm reminded of you, Lord, and how much we can do with your help.
May I remind others of that so we can combine efforts for your glory;
it's so easy to get caught up in our petty, self-centered concerns.

Once again, the song "For Those Tears I Died" (Stevens) comes to mind.
No matter what concerns and sorrows we have, Jesus is with us,
reminding us that his "living water" quenches every thirst.

What About You?

1. What reminds you to take pause and adjust your outlook?

2. What are some reminders that come straight from the Bible? Which one(s) would you like to act on right now?

3. What is the most important thing to keep in mind as we travel through life? How can we best remind ourselves and others of that?

Sense

August 27, 2010

God has truly blessed us with marvelous gifts that money can't buy, such as our five senses: sight, sound, touch, smell, and taste. Of course, we take them for granted—until something happens to make us realize how very precious they are and how much joy they add to our lives. Today, I sensed God telling us to appreciate our many gifts (especially our senses) and to handle them with loving care. And that includes our "sixth sense," that special ability to tap a power that goes beyond the ordinary.

Then there's "common sense," something I need to work on. I'm improving, I know, because I'm now responding to promptings that hold me back from saying or doing certain things, or rushing in "where angels fear to tread!" I'm also deleting things in my outgoing emails that aren't worth saying (and can be held against me!) And what's so great is that the more I listen to these helpful promptings, the more I sense the next ones. My goal now is to establish habits based on these wise directives, so I'll automatically be prudent and discreet without so much nudging.

And finally, there are those things we can't make any sense of at all—like why there's such inequality and hatred in the world, why bad things happen to good people and vice versa. It's those utterly senseless things that are best left in the hands of our omniscient, omnipotent God, so we can put our time and energy into doing what we can (while we can) to add goodness and grace to this hurting world. The more we do that, the more we'll be able to sense God in and around us—and the closer we'll get to those seemingly impossible answers.

I sense your Spirit, Lord—a special gift to get me through the next 3 days.
There's so much to think about and do for our outdoor Dogfest.
There will be food, games, vendors, music, speakers...

No rain is predicted for the event—just extreme heat. Last year we
drowned in the deluge and this year we'll bake. But I won't worry—
I sense you saying: I'll take care of it; just do your part well.

We still haven't finalized the printed program—we keep adding things.
Reporters are calling—at least three or four of them will be coming.
Please don't let me miss anyone or forget something important, Lord!

What About You?

1. I sense that our upcoming Dogfest, which benefits animal rescue, will
    be very successful. What are you now sensing as you open yourself to
    God's Spirit?

2. Three years ago I felt God directing me to adopt our dog, Jessie. She
    is now a therapy dog and the inspiration for our charitable events.
    When have you followed an inner prompting that changed lives for
    the better?

3. What can we do to "set the scene" and make it easier to sense God's
    promptings?

Reap

August 29, 2010

After eating, sleeping, and breathing dogs for the past two or three months, our big Dogfest 2010 finally arrived. The time for sowing is past. Now we'll see what sort of a harvest our efforts have generated. Already I have a lot to be thankful for. I was blessed with a calm spirit both last night and this morning. So, I got some quality sleep and faced the day peacefully and confidently. We also had no rain this year, which was a true blessing. Last year we got rained out part way through. Today was hot—in the nineties—but no humidity and lots of shade in the park.

The proof of really being organized would be to leisurely watch Joel Osteen on TV at 9:00, but not this year! Dogfest officially started at 1:00, but people were coming by 10:30 to help us rake the uneven woodchips and set everything up. I left Hugo home to wait for Julie and Curt's trailer to pick up our big stuff, and I drove to the park to start with the set-up. Things were looking really good...until we couldn't find the 400 yellow programs that Hugo and I had so painstakingly prepared yesterday. I panicked and drove home to print more, only to realize that my printer was at the park for the education center! I tried to involve God but inside I was too frantic to function or think well.

We finally found the programs at the park—after the event, so no one knew what was happening and when. I also goofed with the music for the parade and the fashion show, and those two events weren't anywhere near what I'd envisioned. Our 40 sponsors couldn't see themselves listed (no programs) and the games and events suffered because people weren't aware of them.

Instead of socializing I rushed around, straining my knee in the process.
The featured dignitary spread political propaganda against our wishes.
But I held up well and had a great time anyway!

Our harvest was plentiful: singers and keyboard players from preteen
to octogenarian, happy dogs and their happy people—and a lot of
interest in the adoptable dogs that the rescue groups brought.

We made good money with our food, drink, games, and books.
The volunteers, helping in every conceivable way, truly saved the day!
And a childhood friend stopped by—with a $100 check!

What About You?

1. One of our vendors, who spent the day making cute sketches of dogs, donated $79 (half of what she took in) to our foundation. When and how have *you* given or received so generously?

2. In John 4:35-38 Jesus says that one person plants and someone else harvests. How have others reaped the benefits of your hard work, and how have you benefited from others' labors?

3. How can we leave some gleanings for others when we reap good things for ourselves? (See Deuteronomy 24:21)

Promise

August 31, 2010

Am I just a harbinger of gloom, or are promises not holding much water these days? My dad always said that a person's word is his or her bond—no need to even put it in writing. Today, pre-nuptial agreements and hundred-page insurance policies (like our one-day event insurance contract for Dogfest) are evidence that we're living in a world where we had better assume the worst. I've become so insecure and untrusting that I keep reminding people and micro-managing them, for fear they won't fulfill their commitments. And when people do what they say they'll do I'm very impressed. Perhaps it's my own weakness in this area that prompts me to act this way.

This past year I've been striving to be the person I want others to be—one who follows through on promises and does things in a timely, conscientious fashion. But I still fall far short. And when I let people down (sometimes seemingly on purpose) I feel so badly. I know, for example, that I let a lot of folks down at Dogfest because I didn't follow through on what was promised. One vendor ended up with a bad placement and a hassle with the rented table and chairs. And those anxiously awaiting the doggie dress-up and parade were sorely disappointed.

How can I do better, Lord? Like Paul, I lament that even when I know what I should do, I so often fail to do it. (Ro 7:14-24) Sometimes I even thwart my own good intentions and hard work. I know that my answer comes in verse 25, when Paul concludes: *Thank God! Jesus will rescue me!* (from myself!) I'm also comforted by his wonderful words in Phil 4:4-13 that end with: *I can do all things through Christ who strengthens me.*

I'm grateful that your promises are sure, Lord--not like our human ones.
Our promises are so flimsy. James reminds that our lives here on
earth are fleeting, and so much is uncertain. (4:13-15)

Since we know so little about tomorrow James tells us not to make
vows (5:12) and to add "Lord willing" when we speak about the future.
I think our worst offense is making a promise we know we won't keep.

We promise to be faithful in marriage, to raise our children in the
faith, and to do Christ's work as we travel through life.
Help us, Lord, to keep all of our promises.

What About You?

1. I promise to always remember my goal/mission/purpose in life: to draw closer to God each day and bring others closer, too--all for God's glory. What promise(s), large or small, are you striving to honor today?

2. The verse about Christ enabling us (Phil. 4:13) gives me the patience and courage to keep moving in the direction I want to go. Which of God's and Jesus' promises do you find most comforting and empowering?

3. What comes to mind as good examples of promises kept?

Orchestrate

September 1, 2010

Well, now that our big Dogfest event is over, I see that my orchestration skills leave a lot to be desired, so I'm not surprised that this word has cropped up. As usual, I bit off more than I could chew. The only good thing is that with so many things supposed to have happened at Dogfest, at least some went really well. Unfortunately a number of things went wrong—both huge and small (and everything in between). Good things included great press coverage and lots of attention to adoptable dogs and the cause we were fostering—which is very important and something that the dozens of people who helped out can be very proud of.

The list of things going wrong was topped by my losing the box of 400 beautiful programs that would have kept people informed and given well-deserved pats on the back to those who donated and sponsored the event, as well as those participating. That was a horrible thing. Naturally I feel badly about the things that fell short of expectations, but when I think of the wonderful people and dogs that got some good from the day I'm very much comforted.

I sent out a survey to all involved and am getting back some candid comments tempered by congratulations and some very practical ideas for a better Dogfest next year. My goal is to step down more and not try to orchestrate everything. I want Dogfest to belong to the dogs and those who love them. I want to gradually let go and enable capable people to take over and run with it. Of course I'd love to remain part of the "orchestra," helping as I can and spreading joy on the day of the event while watching everything go smoothly, like a well-tuned orchestra!

I like to create big events--a lot of work for a lot of people, says Hugo!
Remember those original plays we did with the third-graders, Lord?
And the full-school production I orchestrated when the school closed?

We did 17 children's choir shows, and two Good Book Player productions.
We dramatized a chapter from Jessie's book, and now Dogfest.
Some ideas were better than others — all were good learning experiences.

But along with the good I can't help but recall pain attached to, even
caused by, my efforts. Tears fill my eyes as I beg to first of all do
no harm, then remember to put people above things--even big things!

What About You?

1. All too often I hurt rather than help people. So, I'm more ready
    than ever before to let God do the orchestrating! Is there anything
    in *your* life that's needs to be more God-directed?

2. Sincere and well-intentioned efforts are often fraught with
    challenges and hurt feelings—it's part of our imperfect human
    condition. But it's important that we not give up doing good works.
    What examples and thoughts do you have in this regard?

3. What are some ways in which people, with God's help, have
    brought good out of even the most miserable of human situations?

Overlook

September 3, 2010

William James (1842-1910), called the father of American psychology, is credited with saying "Wisdom is learning what to overlook." It is indeed healthy to pursue that which is worthy of our time and energy, and to ignore that which can drag us or others down. Overlooking does not necessarily mean forgetting something unpleasant, or not learning from it, for even the smallest negative can carry within it big and practical lessons.

Jesus warned us *not* to overlook the weak, the vulnerable, the "least among us." At one point, he held a child close and told his followers that when they welcome one so small in his name, they welcome him—and when they welcome him, they welcome the One who sent him. (Mark 9:37). On another occasion, he told a story about the final judgment and how we'll be separated on the basis of how we treat those who are ill, in prison, thirsty, hungry, naked... He even equated our treatment of those generally overlooked, to our treatment of him: *Whatever you did (or did not do) to my people, you did (or failed to do) to me. (Matthew 25:31-46)*

A good type of overlooking is when we overlook a perceived slight by someone, or a weakness in a person, or even something we've done that we've already dealt with and learned from. When we refuse to let go of the "rain" in our lives and not let it roll off us like water off a duck's back, we all too easily become bitter or depressed or harbingers of negativity. A wonderful person I know has so much bad to say about others that whenever I mention a person or group I cringe in anticipation of how my opinion will soon be poisoned by this person's opinion.

*Help me, Lord, to know what to overlook as I live each day. Jesus could
easily have overlooked Bartimaeus and the hunched-over woman,
but he heard the man's call and sought out the woman in need.*

*Paul overlooked divisive things in order to preach the Gospel to many,
yet he pinpointed problems and chided people when necessary.
Peter suggested that love helps us cover (overlook) sins.*

*I'll overlook inconsequential things and things that can lead me astray.
I'll not overlook things and people that need God's healing touch,
no matter how inconsequential they may seem to me or to others.*

What About You?

1.   What are some things we can learn to overlook—things that cause un-
     necessary dissension?

2.   Let's also notice (and do) little things that others may miss: the kind
     word, the well-earned praise, the person sitting in the corner...What
     examples of little niceties and random acts of kindness come to *your*
     mind?

3.   How might we be overlooking God as we go about our everyday
     affairs? How can we better see, honor and include the Lord in the
     "everydayness" of our lives?

Emulate

September 4, 2010

As I was growing up, I had plenty of heroes—cowboys like Gene Autry and Roy Rogers, clever detectives like Charlie Chan, and young, adventuresome people like Frankie Darrow and the Bowery Boys. The movies and television were full of good people who never cursed or got involved sexually—and always won out over evil. I also grew up thinking my parents were perfect, too. As I grew and realized that life was not like I'd been led to believe, it upset me, to say the least. But unlike so many, I still to this day consider my parents amazingly wonderful in every way. They lived modest but great lives, and died with dignity, very much loved by family and friends.

People we admire and emulate are bound to fall from their pedestals, or at least tilt the pedestal a bit—but my number-one hero, Jesus, never disappoints me. In fact, he keeps growing more and more perfect as I learn more and more about him and draw closer to him.

A few years ago I wrote a booklet called *Following Jesus Today and Every Day, 52 Ways to Walk in his Footsteps.* It's a simple little booklet, divided into six sections: *Have Faith Like Jesus, Grow in Strength and Wisdom, Be a Doer of the Word, Be Honorable and Genuine, Savor Life's Priceless Blessings,* and *Stay Focused.* It fell together nicely during my early morning walks, with God's Spirit helping me to write it, and now live it. A church in Florida uses it in it's prison ministry. We must make time to get it into more hands because we all need a Savior to emulate.

210

Who is out there emulating us? Probably a lot more people than we realize. Life is short. Now is a good time to check out the values our words and actions reflect to those who observe and interact with us.

Thanks, Jesus, for coming to earth and showing us how to live and love. You understand when we try to walk on water like you—and start sinking as Peter did (Mt 14:25-33). You're ready to help us, too.

Peter, John and Paul were given power to heal people as you did. You told your disciples they'd do even greater things than you did (Jn 14:12). Now we want to emulate them and live for you, as they did.

What About You?

1. Who do *you* emulate? And who do you suspect is emulating you?

2. Why do you think Jesus was so hard on the religious power-people of his day? What are some of the things he said to these people?

3. Who are some of the people throughout history (and in your own life) who deserve to be emulated? Why? Of all those who have ever lived, which one would you most like to meet in person?

Spend

September 5, 2010

Today is Sunday and in keeping with our newly instituted rule to take Sunday as a day of rest...I'm trying to spend it in relaxing, enjoyable ways. A morning at church topped my list: taking communion and seeing people I haven't seen in awhile. I even lessened my chore of returning the chairs we borrowed for last week's event by asking a few of the church men to help me carry them from my car to the church basement. And, I even grabbed a few cookies—not so good, I guess, but fun anyway.

I didn't rush after church, but spoke with the guest pastor about the word *spent*, and how this past week I felt good looking at myself in a mirror. My baggy skin and deep wrinkles are indeed evidence that I've been *spending* myself by working hard at projects to which I feel called. Looking one's age is fine, as long as the years have been well spent.

I think of the Apostle Paul, and how he poured himself out as a living sacrifice, spreading the Good News, setting up and monitoring churches, and finally being martyred like so many others. I have such an easy life compared to Paul and our spiritual forebears, yet I can take their writings and examples and apply them to my life. I, too, can willingly and lovingly "spend" myself doing God's work here on earth. But today is Sunday, so I will sit back, lie down, read, chat on the phone, go out walking, and not worry. I'll spend today with those I love—including the God who has prepared this special day for me, and blessed me so richly.

We can spend our time and money only once. When they're gone, there's
no reclaiming or recapturing. Help me to spend my assets wisely, Lord.
I grieve for opportunities lost, but rejoice in time well spent.

The prophet Isaiah reminds us that God's greatest gifts are freely given.
In 55:1-3 he says: "Why waste your money on what really isn't food?"
Why work hard for something that doesn't satisfy?"

Thank you, Lord, for knowing and meeting our needs. Increase our faith.
Help us to tap that limitless reservoir of good things you have in
store for those who joyfully spend themselves in your service.

What About You?

1.   How are you spending your time, your money, *yourself*?

2.   What are some examples of people who have spent themselves and
     given their all for causes far bigger than themselves?

3.   How do you spend your Sabbaths?

Grasp

September 7, 2010

We can grasp things with our minds as well as our hands. Today I did my best to grasp hold of the responsibilities I feel are mine at the moment—to wrap up the loose ends from the Dogfest (the financial entries, the thank yous, etc.) and to move ahead with the upcoming Book Launch. Other things vied for my time and attention, however—such as getting to the supermarket early to grab some great sales items. And how could I refuse the opportunity to eat at our favorite buffet en route to meeting with our financial planner?

Of course we had to pick up a few things at Trader Joe's market on the way home, and then our dog Jessie needed a walk in the sunshine on this gorgeous day. A chat with our daughter Elisa and family left the day well-rounded as it slipped right through my fingers like a receding wave at the seashore.

Time cannot be grasped—it runs free and stops for no one. But I *can* grasp Hugo's hand and tell him how much he means to me right now. And I can grasp every opportunity to add a little joy to another's life. Tonight I wrote checks to refund some money to the animal rescue groups that participated in Dogfest—and along with the check I sent a photo of them at the event. I'm sure they'll appreciate both the refund and the extra thought that went into sending the photo.

I may not grasp the meaning of life and many of its ups and downs, but, as the song says, "I know who holds the future and I know who holds my hand." And no matter what, I won't loosen my grip; I won't let go!

*The woman with the long-endured illness had tried everything...
except taking hold of Jesus. The remedy to good health is still to
grab hold of Jesus, even if all's well (He makes good even better!)*

*According to poet Robert Browning, our reach should exceed our grasp so
we stretch toward something big. "Or what's a heaven for?" he asks.
Like Paul, I reach toward the prize of an eternity with our Lord.*

*Despite my comfortable, blessing-filled life, I still have times when
I'm afraid, depressed, uneasy... but the more I tighten my grasp on
Jesus, the better I combat those intruders when they come my way.*

What About You?

1. How can having a good grip on Jesus make all the difference in our lives?

2. What goals are you now striving for (or would you like to strive for) that are not yet within your grasp?

3. When have you, or someone you know of, reached out to Jesus? How did it work out?

Contemplate

September 8, 2010

It's surprising that this word didn't crop up sooner—it's a very special word for me. More than a decade ago our wonderful Pastor, John Danner, introduced us to contemplative prayer. It was an experience that changed my spiritual life drastically. We sat still, basked in the presence of the Lord, and imagined a God far bigger and more encompassing than I had theretofore ever even considered. As a homework assignment we read the story of blind Bartimeaus (Mark 10:42-52) a couple of times a day, then wrote about it from various perspectives. What an amazing experience!

After searching for awhile I was able to locate my contemplative prayer journal amid several journals full of heartfelt writings related to Bible studies, retreats, courses, and the like. Here is one of the several writings related to our contemplative reading of the Bartimaeus story (written on November 4, 1997):

Today I imagined myself, not as the blind beggar receiving the miracle, but as one of the crowd, in awe of all Jesus has said and done. I seek to know more, to stay close, and along with others I crowd in on him. My single-mindedness is interrupted by the wailings of that ragged underling, Bartimaeus. I hush him and try to squelch his obnoxiousness, but the more I do that the louder and more obnoxious he becomes. I'm shocked when Jesus calls him forward and asks what he can do for him. I'm ashamed when I see the change (both physical and inwardly) in the beggar, and I realize that Jesus' love does not discriminate against the ill, the weak, the downtrodden, the lowly. I ask for a miracle, too— that I can also love equally and unconditionally—and thus be healed of the attitudes that separate me from him. As I write this I can see Jesus calling me and asking the same question, and then granting my desire while saying lovingly, "Go, your faith has healed you."

*Contemplative prayer drew me closer to God than ever before, or since.
One morning during that time I awoke early singing a new song.
I jumped up, wrote it down and hummed it into a tape recorder.*

*It was a loving message from God to all of us: Time with me (repeat),
beloved child, spend some time with me. I love you so but there's
no way you'll know unless you spend a little time with me.*

*Six verses flowed from my heart onto the paper—a lovely song
about spending time with God and staying close to him. We've
sung it at church and on retreat, with either piano or guitar.*

What About You?

1. To contemplate means to look at or think about something steadily, thoughtfully and seriously—at length, in order to understand it more fully. What are you (or should you be) contemplating at this point in your life's journey?

2. Buddha is credited as saying, "As we think, so we become." What are some examples that prove this statement?

3. Jesus spent time alone with God in the early morning silence. What happens when we do the same—and perhaps do some journaling, as I did with the Bartimaeus story?

Acclimate

The days are getting shorter (daylight-wise) and cooler, so it's time to start acclimating again! We'll save a little money by not needing either air conditioning or heat some of the time, and we'll have to start grabbing our jackets when we go out—at least for part of the day.

Life is a constant adjustment to change, and those of us that do it best outlive those that don't do it so well. I recall seeing a documentary about people who live to be at least one hundred years old. They were interviewed and studied to see what factors played into their longevity. It was discovered that the long-lived people stay active and involved in hobbies and activities. They also acclimate well to life's big changes, including tragedies like losing a partner, dear friends, a child, and in some cases even grandchildren.

St. Paul was a master at acclimating. He knew how to be abased and how to abound—and was content in whatever state he found himself. He experienced both extreme hunger and great abundance, yet seemed not to prefer one above the other. The Contemporary English Version quotes him this way: *I am not complaining about having too little. I have learned to be satisfied with whatever I have. (Philippians 4:11)* His secret? Philippians 4:13: *Christ gives me the strength to face anything.* "I'd Rather Have Jesus," sings George Beverly Shea...than anything else!

We don't know what's ahead—and that's good. It frees us to truly enjoy the moment we're in. Jesus warns us not to worry about tomorrow; there's enough to acclimate to today!

218

*Our character is revealed by what we acclimate to. Are we easily swayed
by the world's changing values? Do we always bend to peer pressure?
Do we "buy into" others' opinions without doing our own due-diligence?*

*On the other hand, do we acclimate our lives toward the Lord, following
his precepts, adhering to the Spirit's promptings, and taking Jesus
with us no matter where we go or who we're with?*

*Help me, Lord, to be about your business right here and now.
When changes assail my peaceful world, guide me safely through them.
Mold and remold me so I can acclimate to the ups and downs of life.*

What About You?

1.   How are you when to comes to acclimating to life's big, and little,
     challenges? (Sometimes people say, "I can handle the fires; it's the
     spilled milk that does me in!")

2.   The Holy Spirit helped the disciples to acclimate to Jesus' death and
     to move ahead confidently. How has faith helped you and others you
     know (or know of) to move ahead despite hard times?

3.   What is your prayer today—for yourself and for others, especially
     those who are having trouble acclimating?

Honor

September 11, 2010

This is a sad day, a day when we remember those who died so tragically and horrifically nine years ago when terrorists mercilessly murdered almost 3,000 innocent people—of all ages and nationalities. Two of the young people who died in the World Trade Center that morning attended our church. Scott sang in my children's choir as a youngster and Jennifer was in church just two days before the attack. Almost everyone in this area knew *someone* who died that day.

The word *honor* is appropriate because today we should take some time to honor those who died, pray for those who have felt the sting of their deaths most deeply, and remember those who have sacrificed and continue to sacrifice as hatred and violence seem to intensify rather than subside. We ache to change and improve things, but feel so helpless in the shadow of such immense challenges. But something we can all do is *honor*—our parents, our leaders, our God.

It is certainly an *honor* to live in a time when we have such easy access to knowledge and communication (with a loved one on a local errand and with people continents away.) And it's an honor to live in a country that was built on Christian values and, even though it's strayed of late, remains a place where people still believe strongly in a God of love, and have heartfelt compassion for those in need, both people *and* animals. And the biggest honor is being able to read God's Word for ourselves, in any number of translations, enabling us to have a personal relationship with our Creator, who is well aware of the state our world is in, and will act on it when the time is right. Meanwhile we honor his timetable.

*Humble me, Lord, so I'll give honor to others and not seek it for myself,
I'll take the back seat, do the kind thing, respect others' opinions.
I'll stay close to you and humbly accept any honors you bestow on me.*

*I look awfully serious in candid photographs. Loosen me up, Lord. Let me
relax in your arms, honoring and loving you with all my heart...
I'll honor and love Hugo, too, as I promised I would 43 years ago.*

*Today honor is in short supply as our country flounders economically,
environmentally, medically, socially, morally—with so many sides to
every issue. Help us to see the truth as you see it, and live by it.*

What About You?

1. Who are some people, past and present, who deserve most to be honored? Why?

2. What are some ways in which we can honor our parents, our leaders, our God?

3. What are some things we can do to better know and apply God's perspective?

Confess

September 15, 2010

We had quite a few Catholic friends in the Teaneck, NJ, neighborhood where my siblings and I grew up. They went to confession, ate fish on Friday, went to weekday catechism, crossed themselves when they got up to bat, and attended services that were conducted in Latin. We Protestants did none of those things.

Nowadays we're not so different. We seem to be more prone to confessing. Before I married and left Teaneck Methodist I noticed that we were using some of David's repentant Psalms to express our own penitence: *Unto Thee, and Thee only, have I sinned.* I now looked this verse up on my favorite concordance-like Web site, www.SearchGodsWord. org—and sure enough, I found it almost verbatim in Psalm 51:4. In our Congregational United Church of Christ, which I attend now, we have a whole section of the worship dedicated to confession—it always ends with a Prayer of Confession, in unison. And one verse which our Pastor often quotes is (Let's see if I can recall it): *If we say we haven't sinned the truth is not in us.* (A quick search reveals that it's 1 John 1:8: "If we say we have no sin, we deceive ourselves and the truth is not in us.") Pretty close!

I have a lot to confess—I guess we all do. Just this evening, as I walked around the track at the gym, I thought about when I took extra two-for-a-penny candy and the grocer trusted me and never checked. I also thought about when I was a bit older and carved my foot-high initials into the wooden school door. Someone had a knife and I just did it. When I finished, I realized it was a shocking thing that couldn't be undone—and everyone *had* to notice the bright initials against the dark green door.

Soon the principal and other officials were looking and asking about it.
Of course we all lied. And no adult ever thought I'd do such a thing.
They put in a new metal door, and it was forgotten (but not by me).

Since then, I did even worse things that have more directly hurt others.
I did nasty things without admitting them/apologizing. In one case,
I apologized 30 years later, and was both forgiven and thanked!

The person said she took a good look at herself and realized things
that she, too, had done to hurt others. We'll still friends today!
Lord, help me sin less, 'fess up more, and forgive as I've been forgiven.

What About You?

1. What in your life have you yet to confess?

2. When have you (or others) confessed and been blessed?

3. It seems that the more we do and say, the more we have to confess.
    How can we do more good with less collateral damage?

Include

No one was more inclusive than Jesus. He broke down many walls by talking to a foreign woman at the well, touching a leper begging to be healed, and eating with tax collectors! I'm sure he would even have drawn a circle to include those he so often chided—had *they* been open to changing their thoughts and actions. Nicodemus, a member of the religious elite who opposed Jesus, snuck out one night to speak with Jesus… and this encounter resulted in those marvelous Scriptures about being born again, God sending his Son into the world not to condemn it but to save it—and the best known of all Scriptures, John 3: 16: *God so loved the world that he sent his only begotten Son that whosoever believes in him should not perish, but have everlasting life.*

We can follow the spiritual growth of Nicodemus who, after this encounter, tried to protect Jesus without letting on that he was a believer (John 7:37-52). Later, we find Nicodemus not worrying about what others might think of him or do to him as he helped Joseph of Arimathea, also emboldened by a growing faith. Together they took Jesus' body from the cross, applied the spices brought by Nicodemus, and laid Jesus' body in a borrowed tomb. (John 19:38-42)

I pray for an inclusive attitude that brings people together and helps us know and understand the God who created and loves us. This evening, we had a "Happy Birthday, All!" party for the little girls at a Children's Aid group home. My friend, Lisa, and her teenage daughters raised money at a yard sale to give the little ones a pizza and beading party. They made lovely beaded bracelets and took home goody bags of fun things that hadn't sold at Lisa's garage sale.

Eight little ones of different ages and races were included.
Open Doors matched the garage sale proceeds for more fun times--
to include opportunities for them to give as well as receive.

I like Edwin Markham's little poem filled with big wisdom: "Outwitted."
"He drew a circle that shut me out—heretic, rebel, a thing to flout.
But love and I had a wit to win: We drew a circle that took him in!"

A young man with a mental health challenge volunteered at Dogfest.
His taking part was good for him, his dog, and all who attended. He
was a big help and was even quoted by a reporter covering the event.

What About You?

1. Who is the most inclusive person you know? Why?

2. When have you not felt included? When have you not included someone? Looking back, how could you have positively influenced those situations?

3. Years ago I said yes to an irritating colleague who needed a ride to work each morning. She turned out to be a wonderful person and I'm so glad I got to know her. What happy inclusion stories can *you* tell?

Befriend

September 25, 2010

Today a friend inspired the word! She came (at just the right time, fully prepared and ready to help—much like an angel or the Lone Ranger. She loaded her SUV with my gazebos, Jessie's waggin' wagon of books and materials, and lots of other stuff. Then she drove me and my stuff to the center of town and helped to unload it and set everything up so our non-profit, Open Doors, could be part of our town's first Sidewalk Sale. It was a long, hot day—starting with a walk with Jessie, then my falling at home as I walked carrying stinky canned salmon and a dish of water for the cat. Fortunately I didn't hurt myself too badly, and my friend soon arrived and told me to take an aspirin to prevent my injured leg and shoulder from swelling. She also brought along eyewash to treat Jessie's runny eye.

Yes, the day Julie befriended me (at last year's "Pets and Heroes" event, when she was one of the animal rescue heroes) was indeed a blessed day for me. Since then, she did more than any other helper to make our Dog-fest fun'raiser a big success, welcomed Hugo and me into her home for a barbeque with friends and family, and even wants us to vacation with them on a cruise to Bermuda next April. And she has continued to help in so many ways. And today, she (and her "reading" dog Sierra, who responds to the written words "Sit", "Stay", "Down", and "Come") made a great difference at the benefit Sidewalk Sale. So this was an ideal day to think about good friends like Julie.

Hedy is another whose friendship warms my heart. She prepared delicious food for the party we had when our daughter and family visited. She also helped to set up and to serve.

*Hedy's friendship goes back to when our daughters were pre-schoolers.
She truly lives up to one of her favorite poems: "Make new friends
but keep the old; the first are silver and the others gold."*

*Jesus befriended all kinds of people. He calls us to do the same.
In John 15:1 he says there's no greater love than to lay down one's
life for a friend. That's exactly what he did for us!*

*He also says that our part of the friendship includes our obeying him...
not as servants but as obedient friends. (John 15:13-15)
Help us, Lord Jesus, to be good friends to you and to others.*

What About You?

1. Why do you think the song *What a Friend We Have in Jesus* is a favorite of so many believers? How do *you* consider Jesus to be a friend?

2. What friends stick out in your memory? Who are your closest friends today?

3. When did you befriend someone (or someone, you) in an unusual or special way?

Travel

September 27, 2010

Travel is something I've always enjoyed. It started with our one-week vacations in Ocean Grove, the little Methodist town along New Jersey's stretch of the Atlantic Ocean. Our elderly third-cousins, whom my sister, brother and I called Flossie and Blanche, treated us to these marvelous excursions for a few summers during our formative years. Flossie, especially, loved traveling and would show movies of her trips to Washington DC during cherry-blossom time and a cruise to Bermuda. She even loved taking us by bus into Manhattan to see the Christmas decorations. My poor, hard-working parents never got away much until they were finally retired—then they enjoyed driving to the west coast, taking a cruise, and even owning their own little boat, docked right in their backyard.

I seized the opportunity after my first year of teaching to go on an educational tour of nine countries in four weeks. What an experience! I got to see Paris, London, Madrid, Athens, Innsbruck, Lucerne, Munich, Brussels, and lots of towns in Italy. I still have the journal that I wrote during that trip, when I learned to sleep sitting up in a bus!

My marriage to Hugo opened up more opportunities to travel as I accompanied him on his seminars to Canada, San Francisco, Montana, and other interesting places. And we especially enjoyed the visiting to his mother in Switzerland where she would treat us to a week's vacation somewhere in that gorgeous country. Hugo taught me to ski so we skied there, as well as in Vermont and other areas closer to where we lived, first in NYC and then in New Jersey.

Our greatest trip was when our church group visited the Holy Land.
I always yearned to walk where Jesus walked and see the Biblical sights.
To see it with Hugo and our church friends was a dream come true!

The trip was led by Pastor Danner. And an Israeli archeologist added extra
depth to our experience. I was re-baptized—right in the Jordan River.
And Hugo and I re-married, in Cana, where Jesus turned water to wine.

Now we travel mostly to Florida to see family or enjoy Sanibel, where
Pastor Danner now is. At this stage we realize that it's best to "travel light"
on life's journey and enjoy God's miracles right in our own backyard.

What About You?

1.   What travels have you enjoyed? Where would you still like to visit?

2.   How lightly are you traveling in life? (Hopefully you don't have nearly
     so many things to get rid of as I do!)

3.   What have you learned from your travels, and how can that
     knowledge be used for God's good purposes?

Cut

September 30, 2010

This little word has been doing a big job in my life. I used it a lot yesterday—each time I wanted to grab a sugary snack. It reminded me that I want to cut those things out of my diet. And it worked! That, combined with my early morning imaging of God cutting the cords that bind me to earthly things, has kept me from eating any "serious" sugar for two days now. Serious sugar would be those yummy chocolate-dollop cookies or a package of M&Ms, or a bar of chocolate. I did have some less-serious sugar: gluten-free pancakes with fresh berries, condensed apple juice and a little maple-agave syrup.

Today I took a step further in the right direction by actually throwing away the remainder of the potato chips I recently bought, and have been dipping into whipped cream cheese. So, candy, cookies, and now potato chips are being cut out of my lifestyle. This has happened before. Perhaps this time I'll maintain it as a healthy habit. I'll have to pretend I'm directing a movie and have the authority to yell "Cut!" whenever I want or need to. It's also helpful for editing my outgoing emails--cutting out that which is unnecessary, self-centered, boring, too easily misunderstood, etc.

Hugo recently told me to be less negative in the way I speak—and a couple of times I caught *him* being the guilty party. It certainly helps to have a "buddy" to assist in this constant "pruning." We just have to remember to be gentle and encouraging with each other (and with ourselves) as we go through these "growing pains." The biggest help is having God in the equation—with God's help the growth can be multiplied many times over.

*Things to cut: interrupting people, not covering my cough, and putting
my projects/needs/interests/etc. above others'—to name just a few.
What else? Hurrying, being late, and getting behind in my paperwork.*

*What to increase (not cut): time with the Lord and interest in others.
More things to cultivate: my attentiveness toward Hugo,
my reliability, my ability to communicate well—to name just a few.*

*Thank you, Lord, for helping me to better prune and fertilize my life.
I look forward to less TV, a more balanced workload, and soon an
upcoming Florida vacation so we can enjoy our loved ones there.*

What About You?

1. What most needs to be cut down (or cut out) in your life?

2. Conversely, what needs to be nourished and increased in *your* life?

3. On both a personal and a global scale, what do you think God
    most wants us to eliminate, reduce, and/or magnify?

Detach

October 1, 2010

Today I knew our word early on. In fact, I used it in my "imaging" before I even got up. I "saw" and felt myself being lifted up, bathed in God's love and detaching from everything. One after another, the cords that were tugging at me fell away from me. Yesterday (in conjunction with the word *cut*) I saw God's loving hand doing the cutting to remove those things that cling to me and hold me back; but today I worked *with* God, detaching and letting go, sometimes even before God got to cut the cords. Interestingly, not everything could be cut or released—a very liquid coating that totally surrounded me, united again, and went upward, was unyielding.

This is what I wrote in my journal when I got up: *I saw myself clipped of the cords that were tying me to things and people—only the connection to God remained. It was a fluid connection, filling in the rough spots that stuck out after the "pruning," locking in the essence of the people and dreams I'd detached from, and healing any wounds from the resentments, shames, and unhealthy ties that had been cut. No matter how often or strongly I tried to cut the tie that bound me to God, it couldn't be done. The clippers/scissors would go right through it, leaving the connection to God unbroken.*

I shouldn't be surprised at this because the Bible tells us that nothing can separate us from the love of God—nothing in this world or beyond this world. (See Ro 8:35-39). I then continued my journaling: *It's a great feeling to know that nothing/no one is as unchanging, important, or powerful as our loving Creator.*

*Letting go of loved ones doesn't mean that we lose them. We just
have to offer them to the Lord, as Abraham did with Isaac. With God
as our sustainer, we gain back much more than we release (Ps 37:4).*

*Just because I detach from my dreams doesn't mean they're lessened or
pushed away. In fact, the more I let go of good things the greater
the chance they'll be drawn to my confidence and objectivity.*

*It's the unimportant, destructive, deceptive things that will slack off
and be kept at bay. This is where God's protective love becomes
a barrier between us and what can hurt or hinder us.*

What About You?

1.   I've been described as driven and determined, but my goal now is to
     be called "calm accepter." How have *you* been described, and what
     would you now *like* to be called?

2.   What are some good (and not-so-good) things and people that you
     should release into God's hands? Which do you expect would then
     draw closer, and which would probably fall away?

3.   How can God help us (and we help others) to cling less and less to the
     people and things around us, and more and more to the things of God?

Build

October 7, 2010

Billy Graham has been a great evangelist for generations. He's the greatest one ever in my opinion, because he's the one who drew our entire family forward to claim Jesus as our Lord. There's something very powerful and wonderful about walking forward to declare one's faith. I was just thirteen years old then, and I can still feel a touch of the buoyancy and euphoria I felt then as I recall how I glided down tier after tier of Yankee Stadium steps in order to get to that huge field with thousands of others, all wanting the same thing: to draw closer to the God so aptly described by this great orator (pause to wipe tears).

I guess it's not surprising that one of the books I'm presently reading is his latest, *The Journey*, written as he looks back on his many years of service to the Lord. And early this morning, as I read the section called "Preparing for Adversity" (in the chapter titled "When Life Turns Against Us"), I was once again inspired by this great man of God. In fact, he inspired our Word-of-the-Day: *build*. He says that now is the time to build a spiritual foundation that won't collapse under the weight of life's reverses. I've tried my whole life to stay as close to God as I can because I'm a coward. I know that pain and heartache are part of being human, and when things get unbearable I want to have a close relationship with the only One who can do something about it and get me through it.

Dr. Graham says to *Remember your Creator in the days of your youth, before the days of trouble come (Ec12:1)*, so your strong connection to God will carry you through any and all of life's challenges.

234

Jesus contrasts a wise person with a foolish person in Mt 7:24-25.
A wise person builds a house on rock (hears and obeys him).
A foolish person builds a house on sand (hears but doesn't obey him).

I'd like to build up our assets again so we can have a condo in Florida
and still stay here in New Jersey for half of the year. I also want to
build up Open Doors so our Kids'n'Kritters project will materialize.

And I'd dearly like to build a stronger bond with our daughter, Elisa, by
giving her and baby Jessica quality time. And of course I want to be a
reflection of you, Lord, and build up treasures in heaven.

What About You?

1. What are you building in *your* life? What are you building your life *on*?

2. Consider the story in Genesis 11:1-9 about the Tower of Babel. Why is it important that we check out our motives for doing what we're doing?

3. What are some other ways, in addition to prayer and Scriptures, to build a strong foundation in life?

Strengthen

October 8, 2010

We've been working hard for decades, doing what we can to keep our bodies strong, flexible, and healthy. When we were first married and lived in New York City, we did a lot of walking and even climbed the fifteen flights to our apartment now and then for an extra workout. I sometimes wonder how many "on foot" miles we've clocked together over the years.

In the winter we used to ski, staying fit by controlling our skis on the way down, and carrying our skis as we traipsed around in the snow below. As aging suburbanites, we decided it was time to hit the gym instead of the slopes! We've tried to maintain a 3-times-a-week routine for almost twenty-five years now: swimming, working out, and walking—or in Hugo's case, jogging—on the track. Hugo also likes to do outside jogging. And I've done 5 minutes of back stretches each morning for years to ward off the lower back pain that started in my thirties.

Our efforts to strengthen our bodies have paid off! Hugo (81) and I (almost 67) are doing well. We take no meds—just supplements and some bio-identical hormones. I still can't keep up with Hugo in the gym, but I take the lead in walking. And my back is doing great. Eating well and thinking in a healthy manner has helped a lot, too.

It's good to be physically strong, but it's more important to be spiritually strong. Our word today came to the fore when I found myself telling God about my desire to strengthen my ability to make a decision (or promise) and stick with it.

I'm so quick to change my mind and my stance. I want to be a rock, not a branch blowing in the breeze. A fellow walker at the park today suggested a new location for our Dogfest—and I actually considered it.

I like to please everyone, Lord, but by trying to do that, I please no one. Instead, I hurt people and get myself in trouble, too. Please give me strength and wisdom to be decisive, steadfast, dependable.

Elisa ardently sought inner strength, and you, Lord, have helped her. She and her new family attend church, one of the best ways to to gain the characteristics we all need in order to live for you.

What About You?

1. I would also like to strengthen my ability to keep my mouth shut and my nose out of others' business. What are some inner qualities *you* would like to strengthen?

2. How can God help us strengthen our faith, stamina, and ability to meet life's challenges head-on?

3. Who is your hero or heroine when it comes to the kind of inner strength that plays out in kind, effective words and actions?

Fly

October 9, 2010

When I think of flying I think of time. I'm constantly amazed at how quickly time flies. It seems just a short time ago (and yet, in other ways, so long ago!) that I was a child—then a teenager. And now I'm already a senior citizen.

Our granddaughter Jessica celebrates her first birthday today. That first year is a fly-by miracle. We see a totally helpless infant turn into a bounding toddler having the time of his/her life—as we look on in amazement. And joy of joys! Today was our day to fly! All the way to Florida to see this miracle for ourselves.

I'm writing now from Lake Worth, Florida, where Hugo and I are spending a week enjoying Jessica and her parents, Elisa (our daughter) and Danny. Our flight was perfect—everything went splendidly; smooth flying all the way. We were met by our loved ones and even provided with a car to use. Together we enjoyed a nice beach walk, a healthy buffet at Sweet Tomatoes (a veggie lover's banquet), shopping to stock up on food and supplies, and then the greatest show on earth: our own adorable toddler entertaining us as we just sat there and watched.

Other things that fly by are opportunities that must be grasped now or never. But when I think of God, I'm reminded that we should never say "never." Ours is a God of unlimited chances, a Savior of forgiving "seventy-times-seven," and a Spirit that reaches out to us even when we can't reach out for ourselves.

Opportunities lost can lead to spiritual growth that opens us up to fresh opportunities that could never have come about any other way. The death of Jesus' friend Lazarus is a dramatic example (John 11).

We all want to fly, Lord, and it's amazing how close we are to it. We hang glide, helicopter, jet, and rocket through the skies! Yet earthly problems overwhelm us: hate, fear, pain, injustice...

O Lord, let my life not fly by without enjoying loved ones, helping those in need, and glorifying you. And when it's time to leave this earthly home may I "fly away" in joy and anticipation.

What About You?

1. In what ways have you noticed time flying?

2. What opportunities have you missed? What good has come (and perhaps can still come) from those lost opportunities?

3. I think of Isaiah 40:31 that talks about God giving us new strength to soar like an eagle and not get tired. What are some ways in which we can fly like an eagle and do God's work on earth-- right now, today?

Empower

October 11, 2010

How I'd love to be able to empower others, to subtly help them become self-motivated as they find and apply the very best within themselves. I'd like to make things better rather than worse. It seems to me that all too often I end up hurting people rather than helping them. I either enable them by giving or doing too much (to their, and also to my, detriment) or make them feel worse by saying or doing the wrong things. I also excel at making wrong assumptions about people and situations. Maybe God wants me to improve in this area—how grateful I'd be!

> OK, Lord, where do I start? *Be still and know that I am God. (Psalm 46:10) Let not your heart be troubled. Neither let it be afraid. (John 14:27)*

Maybe I try so hard to help others because I'm afraid—afraid that I'm not good enough, or liked enough, or will end up alone with no one to care or remember me. And I know I'm not quiet enough—my heart is restless; my moods ebb and flow. I go from feeling strong and faithful to feeling weak and guilty. How can I empower someone else?

Of course we all know that God does his best work when people admit they fall short—far short. Even Paul admitted that he did what he hated and didn't do what he knew was right. He says this: *In every part of me I discover something fighting against my mind, and it makes me a prisoner of sin that controls everything I do. What a miserable person I am. Who will rescue me from body that is doomed to die? Thank God! Jesus Christ will rescue me. (Ro 7:14-25)*

240

In Phil 4:13 Paul tells us what empowered him to spread the Gospel and start the first Christian churches. His words have certainly inspired me: *"I can do all things through Christ who strengthens me."*

Paul proves that in order to empower others _we_ must be empowered by the only One who is able to put us to good use despite our human frailties. Right now I feel touched by the same Spirit that touched Paul.

If my motives for helping others are to feel good myself or look good to others, I'll empower no one. I must forget about myself and see others through God's eyes so I can connect them to the Source.

What About You?

1.   What battles are *you* fighting with yourself?

2.   What/who empowers you the most?

3.   How successful are you at empowering others? How might you improve—or help others (like me) become more successful in this fine art of truly helping others?

Connect

October 12, 2010

Today was a great day for a positive word like *connect*. We're here in sunny Florida staying in a nice "boutique hotel"—a modest but clean and cozy place that was a real bargain. Our loved ones are less than a half hour away, so today (our daughter Elisa's 36th birthday) we connected with her and our adorable granddaughter, Jessica, and spent most of the day with them. We enjoyed going to their "Mommy and Me" class in the morning—precious little ones and their moms having a fun time with songs, stories, and lots of action (a program offered free of charge by a nearby Baptist church). Most exciting was when the moms fluffed up the colorful "parachute" for the little ones to run beneath. Of course we got some good photos!

It's so nice to see the various connections Elisa has made during her first year or two in this area. She has helped to bring Danny and his loved ones closer together—in fact, his "mom" (the woman who raised him from age 9) lives in the mother part of their mother-daughter set-up. Elisa and Danny have also attracted nice friends. Evelyn left the area and gave them beautiful furniture; the woman next door gave them her deceased mother's car (the one we're using this week) and also made the delicious lasagna we enjoyed for lunch today. Danny's "sister," now visiting their mom, babysat for Jessica this afternoon while we took Elisa to the movies for her birthday—something Elisa loves to do but rarely gets to do.

Tomorrow we'll connect with a Swiss friend we haven't seen in decades. Ria happens to be vacationing in Lake Worth now, too. A wonderful coincidence!

242

The next day we'll enjoy the zoo with our daughter and her friend.
That's the friend who helped to bring Jessica into the world a year ago.
Thanks, dear Lord, for blessing us with so many healthy connections.

Please connect us, Lord, with people of faith to ease our way.
And connect us to those who can learn and gain from us, too.
Lk 6:38 tells us how much we gain when we give generously!

Most of all, connect us to you, Lord, to give our lives meaning and our
deaths a quantum leap in your direction. As our days dwindle down to a
precious few let us fear not, for we know to Whom we are connected.

What About You?

1.   Whom did you (or whom do you plan to) connect with today?

2.   How have you and God connected over the years? How can you draw
     closer going forward?

3.   Our amazing world of technology enables us to communicate and
     connect with others so easily and in so many different ways. What are
     some pros and cons of these new technologies?

Bridge

October 14, 2010

Earlier this week I had a vivid dream. I was writing a book, and it was completely finished except for the last chapter. All that I could find of that section was a sketch of a bridge. I wasn't worried because I knew I could retrieve the final chapter on my computer. An interesting dream, isn't it? And in that same dream was my teenage boyfriend, Dave, whose impact on my life has been long-lasting. Our relationship went from junior high school right through to our junior year of high school, with time out in the middle. He was very good to me, kind and generous, but I was mean to him. For some yet unknown reason I was mean to a number of people who didn't deserve it, especially at that time in my life—something a psychologist would have a field day with, I'm sure. I did write Dave a letter of apology about 20 years ago that helped me to finally "let go" of the guilt I carried. But I still dream of him on occasion.

Upon awakening from this dream I felt that the bridge symbolized the crossover from this world to the next—that I may not have time to finish all I want to, but that's OK because the rest of the story will be told (not via the computer, but) in heaven. There I will find full closure, not only on the earthly tasks I hope to accomplish but also with the people I have alienated and hurt along the way. Meanwhile, I'm to be a bridge-builder and bring as much reconciling grace into the world as I possibly can. Many people have gaping holes in their lives—both obvious and skillfully concealed. Since I have no way of knowing who needs what, I must depend on God's Spirit to help me bridge the gaps in others' lives, perhaps without even realizing it. By being kind, encouraging, and uplifting whenever I can, gaps will be filled—especially in *my* life.

*Thanks, Lord, for the greatest bridge—Jesus Christ, our Savior, whose
outstretched arms bridge the gap that separates us from you. Thanks
also for bridging the gaps and smoothing the rough spots in my life.*

*Today's word tells me to be a bridge, too, connecting others to you.
Soon I'll be back home in NJ, starting a new chapter in my life.
Jessie and I will work on a sequel to Bark Up the Right Tree.*

*Please help me to glorify you by doing all my projects with great love.
Mother Theresa said we don't have to do great things—just small things
with great love. Please inspire and empower me to follow her advice.*

What About You?

1. When has your kindness to others ended up being an even bigger
    blessing to *you* than to them?

2. Jesus called the peacemakers blessed and happy. What peace-making
    bridge builder do you most admire?

3. Jesus is the way, the truth and the life—he's the narrow road open to
    all 24/7. How can the way we think and act increase the likelihood
    that we (and others) will find, and take, that road?

Return

October 16, 2010

Today we returned home from our week of relaxation in Florida. We had a great time getting to know our little granddaughter, Jessica, who's now walking around and into everything. And it was fun spending time with our daughter, even treating her to a movie for her birthday. Eating at our favorite Golden Corral buffet is always fun, too—albeit fattening. But no matter how delightful our vacation is, it's always nice to come back home—especially with a dog and cat awaiting our return.

As John the Baptist prepared the people for the coming of Jesus, he told them: *Turn back to God and be baptized! Then your sins will be forgiven. (Mark 1:4)* When Jesus finally came, was baptized by John, and spent forty challenging days in the wilderness, his message was similar to John's: *The time has come! God's kingdom will soon be here. Turn back to God and believe the good news! (Mark 1:15)* In both cases it's critical that people return to God in order to be forgiven and to accept the good news that Jesus is our infallible link to a loving Father.

Going back is always hard, because things change and we can never fully recapture the essence of the memories we hold so dear. I still dream about my childhood home and our old neighborhood, but whenever I drive by I'm so out of place now—both it and I have changed so much. But the wonderful thing about God is that he doesn't change. I love what James says in 1:17: *Every good and perfect gift comes down from the Father who created all the lights in the heavens. He is always the same and never makes dark shadows by changing.* No matter how far we stray or how much we change, we can always return to the Lord and feel right at home!

Isn't it amazing how salmon return to their place of birth?
You, Lord, have knit us together in our mothers' wombs,
so our destination in life is to return to you.

Even if we, like salmon, must swim upstream and travel great distances,
we relentlessly strive to be "reborn" spiritually (John 3:1-21).
Only your Spirit can truly bring us home and fill our voids.

Your children, the straying Israelites, were welcomed back whenever
they returned to you. Thanks for doing that for us, too, so that
each time we return we'll be stronger and less likely to stray again.

What About You?

1. When and how have you strayed from (and returned to) God? What are your thoughts and feelings looking back at those experiences?

2. What are some other examples (in nature, history, the Bible, etc.) of the "homing instinct" in action?

3. If you could, what are some people, places, memories, or special feelings you'd like to return to for a quick (or not so quick) visit?

Question

Our former pastor, John Danner, always told us that God doesn't expect us to leave our brains (and our questions and doubts) at the door when we come to church. It's good for us to think through our faith and accept it intellectually as well as emotionally. No one questioned God more than the man who was the "apple of God's eye," David. Jesus even quoted one of David's most heartfelt questions (Psalm 22:1): *My God, my God, why have you forsaken me?* My favorite "David" question is the two-parter he asks: *Where can I go from your Spirit? Where can I flee from your presence? (Psalm 139:7)* when he realizes just how close God is, no matter what.

Jesus commented to his disciples, *You know the way to where I'm going. (John 14:4)* Thomas questioned it: *No, we don't know where you're going. How can we know? (14:5)* Thomas may be known as a doubter, yet he's the one who encouraged the others to accompany Jesus on a dangerous mission to help Lazarus who was dying—in fact, had already died. Thomas boldly said: *Come on, let's go, so we can die with Jesus. (11:16).* And when Thomas kneels at Jesus' feet and says *My Lord and my God! (20:28)* we can feel the strength of his hard-earned faith.

People often ask God: *How can you let needless tragedies like this happen? Why do bad things happen to good people?* And, conversely, they ask: *How could you make such an amazing world and give us such amazing bodies? How can you love us so? Why me, Lord?* A song recorded by people like Elvis, Johnny Cash, the Gaithers, and Kris Kristofferson asks this question: "What have I ever done to deserve even one of the pleasure I've known?" Along with them, I say "Thank you, Lord. I don't have to know all the answers; my comfort comes from knowing that you're in full control."

Our Bible Studies were called "Scripture a Week to Make Us Strong,"
with annual topics like "Favorite Scriptures," "Lessons to Live By," and
"Finding Answers through Biblical Questions."

Today's writing will be part of a faith-building course for
people to "Come Grow with Me" by pondering questions. So I'll
continue this discipline despite Hugo's suggestion to cut it short.

If I feel the need to question or complain, I can go to the Lord as David
did in some of his songs (Psalms). But in general, I'm expecting good
to come—even from our failures and disappointments.

What About You?

1. What more-productive questions can replace ones like "What did I do to deserve this?" or "How can a loving God let this happen?"

2. What question will you ask God when you finally see him face to face as Paul describes in I Corinthians 13:12?

3. Hugo is my question-man, always inquisitive and curious. How can these qualities be used to enrich others' lives as well as the asker's?

Reason

October 19, 2010

This nudge to use my *reasoning* capacity is probably because I too often "shoot from the hip" and make big decisions based on emotions rather than on well-thought-out, objective data. And although Hugo comes across as being much more "reasonable" he's as bad as I am. The fact that we married after just six months (and perhaps a dozen dates) should have been a sure give-away that we'd be doubly-inclined to make hasty decisions as a couple. Some impetuous actions (like getting married to each other and buying certain properties) worked out well. But succumbing to expensive courses and buying *other* properties turned out miserably.

We both also have the tendency to be foolishly generous. I made gifts and loans to people who didn't deserve them and/or never paid them back. And Hugo gave bonuses to employees who not only didn't appreciate them, but actually were abusive to him. We also kept his business going far longer than we should have, but rather than declare bankruptcy we kept paying the employees and the high rent until we'd done well by everyone but ourselves. Earlier, I signed an agreement to rent office space that we never used, and also paid it in full because, after all, I'd given my word. I've always felt that God blesses us in ways much more important than money, if we do what we know is right even though it might be to our detriment.

And we have been richly blessed! We've been healthy and happy for many years; we've come through some terrifying and difficult times; and even though we'd like to have more money for our retirement, we're content with what we have.

I'm thinking about buying a property again (while the houses/condos in
Florida are so reasonable.) But, I must reason things out before
making this money-related decision—we've been "burned" in the past.

Grant me discernment, Lord, to instantly know all the best answers.
But maybe you want me to do the hard work called "due diligence."
I know you'll be with me either way. You've never disappointed me.

I need to reason things out in a number of areas in my life. You've
given me a good brain and the ability to make good decisions. Together
we can fill my final years on earth with control, reason, joy, and love.

What About You?

1. What stories (personal or otherwise) come to mind when we think about hasty decisions versus well-reasoned ones?

2. When have you sought God's presence and not been disappointed?

3. What needs some extra reasoning in your life today? Have you asked God's help? Isaiah 1:18 starts with: *Come now and let us reason together...*

Don't

October 22, 2010

Odd, isn't it, to have the word *don't* before the word *do*? But then, finding the wisdom in any given word is what our Word a Day is all about. As I walked Jessie this morning I thought of some don'ts, such as "Don't count your chickens before they hatch (Aesop)." And just now I typed the words "*sayings: Don't...*" into the Google search engine and got lots of good quotes, including Henry Wadsworth Longfellow's "Don't cross the bridge till you come to it" and Henry Ford's "Don't find fault— find a remedy." Ones that speak to me (authors unknown) are "Don't have too many irons in the fire," "Don't sweat the small stuff," and "Don't toot your own horn."

I wonder what *don'ts* God has in mind for me today? Don't be too hasty in spending money we don't have, perhaps. Or maybe: Don't bite off more than I can chew; Don't fritter time away; Don't forget to smell the roses, relax with loved ones, encourage others; Don't neglect hubby Hugo; Don't worry about the future; Don't be too hard on myself; Don't listen to the inner voice that thwarts my good intentions; Don't over-(or under-)analyze...

The ten commandments have some important don'ts: Don't worship any other gods, don't make idols, don't misuse God's name, don't murder, commit adultery, steal, bear false witness, or covet. Jesus' don'ts are many: *Don't try to show off; don't blow a loud horn (Matt. 6:1,2), Don't worry about having something to eat, drink or wear" (Matt. 6:25), Don't judge [or] be hard on others (Luke 6:37), Don't be greedy (Luke 12:15), Don't be afraid (Luke 12:32), Don't be surprised! (John 5:28)...*

252

A good rule: Don't assume the worst. See/bring out the best in others.
Help me, dear Lord, to see and bring out the best in myself, too.
Don't be pessimistic is another rule—the future's in God's hands.

I hear God saying "Don't waste time." So I'll do creative work in the AM,
not the PM, when I'm tired. Then I'll use the evening for routine
work. Right now I'll take a little nap—a good use of time… I think.

I also hear: "Don't forget to pray." I recently forgot to pray for a
teenager at our church, recovering from surgery—and my brother, Howard,
still in the hospital. I'll add more prayers to my morning quiet-time!

What About You?

1. I'd like to add "Don't procrastinate" to my list. What do you have on your to-don't list?

2. What are some clever ways in which we can convert don'ts into more positive do's?

3. What changes do *you* plan to initiate after considering today's word?

Recharge

October 29, 2010

Even the well-known "Energizer Bunny" on TV, who advertises the longest-lasting battery, eventually needs a battery change or recharge. I guess I'm due for a recharge, too. When I look at my desk, piled high with papers to be dealt with, and my daily to-do lists (which seem to increase faster than I can scratch the tasks off) I feel exhausted and overwhelmed. Oh, to have the time, energy, and know-how to do all I have to do and want to do, and still "smell the roses!"

I start my day by having some quiet time with God whenever I can—that helps. I write in my journal and involve God in my daily planning and decision-making. I sometimes imagine God's love surrounding and filling me so I can reach out in love to others. Also I apply my "Let Go and Listen (then Do and Step Back Again)" technique—and/or I talk with God as I walk the dog. I sometimes fall asleep as I meditate and listen to God, and before I know it an hour or more has passed. I also tend to lose time early in the morning when I snuggle in bed while Hugo shaves and aerates the house. I think I need to balance my inspiring/recharging time with my go-go-go/action time for optimal results.

I not only need to recharge my physical energy; I also need to strengthen that feeling of well-being that comes when I'm in tune with God's Spirit. The more faith and trust I have, the greater my inner strength, which protects me from outside assaults and gets me through the ups and downs of life. I recall an article I read about orphaned children under the care of very trusting believers. Even a harrying escape during a terrifying bombing didn't make them fearful.

Today Hugo recharged the camera for an upcoming occasion and I recharged the battery in my little portable printer for an upcoming event. Such events recharge me, because interacting with others perks me up.

Our weekly worship service is a "shot in the arm," as are the coffee hours and other church activities. Thanks, Lord, for bringing Pastor Chuck and his wife (and more of your Spirit) into our church.

It's a joy to see what your Spirit can do. I envision the Spirit permeating next week's election, inspiring new and effective input for our nation. May all in leadership positions be continually recharged by You!

What About You?

1. When did you (or someone you know or know of) experience an amazing result because faith and trust were strong?

2. My husband, Hugo, has written a booklet called "Wake Up to Abundant Energy," (See www.energizinglife.com). What are some ways in which you are revitalized and energized at the start of, and/or throughout, the day?

3. The movie, "Life is Beautiful," is about a child in a concentration camp, and how a parent's great love protected that child from the horrors surrounding them. How can keeping our attitudes and beliefs well charged protect us and also help those around us?

Communicate

November 2, 2010

Poor communication is no doubt high on the list of roadblocks that hinder healthy relationships. I'm not surprised to be nudged in the direction of better communication because it hasn't been my forte over the years. I admire those who can get their points across clearly, concisely, and in a kind but firm manner—those who speak the truth in love. Tomorrow is election day, so we've been bombarded with all sorts of miscommunications as people are interviewed and have heated debates in an effort to secure a seat in the Senate or House, or a powerful county position. We're seeing lots of examples of how *not* to communicate well.

Communication is definitely an art, not a science. But we can improve. This past weekend the friend we were so nasty to as children (see September 15 "confess") invited me as her guest for her 50th high school reunion. That's the year my sister graduated (one year ahead of me.) I had a great time being more outgoing and sociable than ever. Of course it was easier now that the competition and cliques (in a class of over 600 students) have pretty much evaporated. We're all just glad to be standing, and in many cases even dancing, at age 68.

Dale Carnegie's classic book, "How to Win Friends and Influence People," helped me to see what is most important in dealing with others—certainly not that I get the upper hand or look good. The "secret" is to be fair, kind, and respectful. It's easier said than done, of course! Hugo and I just had a disagreement with our landscaper regarding his gutter-cleaning and snow-removal programs. I don't think we'd have pleased Dale Carnegie. We have a ways to go…

256

*Later today I faced another potentially volatile situation. I handled it
in a quieter, more mature manner—a big improvement.
Help me, Lord, to carefully watch what and how I'm communicating.*

*Early in our marriage I was self-centered and wanted everything my way.
I even went home to mother briefly, but my wise parents said nothing.
They gave me the time I needed to decide on my own to return to Hugo.*

*I determined to forget about myself and work on making him happy.
The whole dynamic quickly changed and 40 years later we're thriving
and looking back on many years of great communication!*

What About You?

1. How well do you communicate with others? What needs
   improvement, and how might you achieve that?

2. Jesus could see right through people who weren't being genuine,
   sincere, or "on target." Where in the Gospels do we see evidence
   of this? [E.g. when Jesus talked about people making donations
   (Mark 12:41-44) and praying (Luke 18:11-14).]

3. How can we better communicate with God and others?

Outen

November 3, 2010

Here's one of Hugo's creative words. It's not unusual for him to ask me to please *outen* the light—or ask me if I *outened* the dog. I'm sure God has a sense of humor and enjoys this word as much as we do. After all, he's using my agnostic husband to bring us both closer to him—that's certainly a wink-and-grin coup. I wanted to marry a minister and ended up with a professed agnostic. But there's something invigorating about living with a benevolent "devil's advocate" that can strengthen one's faith. With God's help, I fully expect to *outen* that "devil" as we continue on our unique journey together—can't wait to see how God will work *that* out!

What I'd like to *outen* in my life right now are those things that hinder me and negatively affect my relationship with God and others—things that keep me from producing the fruit for which God has been nurturing me... things like the "junk" food I crave and wolf down in huge quantities even though I know it's bad for my health, and the work overload that keeps me in a state of low-level (and sometimes even high-level) anxiety. As I write this I get the distinct impression that I'm not at all overworked. As Pastor Chuck says, "The reward for a job well done, is *more* work!" The message I hear coming through is that I don't have to lessen my work. I can actually do a lot more, and do it better, by just arranging things differently.

I have to *outen*, streamline, combine and perhaps change some things in order to be more efficient with my time. For example, I just decided to have a relaxing take-out Chinese meal for those who helped with my October book launch rather than a more-expensive, time-consuming eat-out meal.

258

I also have to outen my tendency to say yes when I should say no to something.
Conversely, Hugo and I also decided to outen our stay-at home mentality
and attend more fundraising events for good causes.

Success! I just outened my desire to gobble up the rest of the chocolate.
It was supposedly for others but I ate most of it. Today's word
will help me to outen my sugar "monster" and get back in shape.

I'll also "knock off" as much as I can of the work piling up on my desk,
so I'll be ready for the accountant's visit in just two weeks.
Then I'll hack away at the clutter in every drawer, closet, nook…

What About You?

1. What do you need to "outen" in *your* life? How can you do it?

2. Jesus "outened" the moneychangers in order to cleanse God's temple. In 1 Co 6:19 Paul calls our body a temple of the Holy Spirit. What are some ways in which we can cleanse *that* temple?

3. Jesus also "outened" those who doubted he could help the little girl who had died (See Mk 5:25-42), but he kept Peter, James and John with him. How can we nurture our faith so that our doubts and skepticism won't keep us from Jesus?

Recycle

November 4, 2010

OK, Lord, we'll do our best to recycle and be good stewards of this amazing earth you've given us. We already take our hazardous wastes to the community college collection site a couple of times a year, and most weeks we put out a container of either glass & plastic or newspapers & cardboard/magazine/junk mail for pick-up. This week we got our container out too late so we'll take it ourselves to the nearest drop-off place. We used to recycle batteries but now we're told to throw them out in the garbage. Somehow I get the feeling that we're not doing enough...

We have an in-sink garbage disposal, a controversial item. Lately, however, it's not working perfectly so I've been throwing a lot of the peelings in the trash. I just now searched the Internet to find out what's preferable, and I learned that there's no easy or set answer. It depends on where we live and how well our community, water treatment plants, and landfills are prepared to handle our rejects. The best alternative is composting, which my friend Julie does. She is a Science teacher and gives lectures on sustainable energy—I'll ask her some questions about how to best preserve our environment. Way back in my junior high school years I felt drawn toward conservation; of all the clubs offered, only this one interested me. And it's never too late to pursue an interest!

Even our dog Jessie does her part by attempting to cover her excrement with dirt and other debris, but laws now require that we dog-owners pick up the poop. I thought that was going to be a miserable task—I never did it for our childhood dog, Corkey. But it isn't difficult or repulsive at all; it's just a matter of "hand in bag, pick it up, pull bag over filled hand, and tie!"

260

Over-population, depletion of the rain forest, exploitation of people and animals, pollution... The list of challenges goes on and on. It seems overwhelming, but there are many things we can do to help.

Think about the waste we make each day, and what we can do to lessen it. I think of my car, lawn sprinkler, gas fireplace, computer, clothing... Help me, Lord, to give more than I take from the environment.

Let's protect, conserve, and reuse. John (Rev 21:1) sees a new heaven and earth—a great recycling miracle, surpassed only by the best surprise of all: our decomposed bodies being changed into new ones (Co 15:51-7)!

What About You?

1. How are you and others recycling? What more could we be doing?

2. Freecycle.org lets people give away usable items, and swap.com lets us trade items. I stop for garage sales, have a previously married hus-band—and a rescued dog. What are some other ways to recycle, both serious and tongue-in-cheek?

3. God is the Great Recycler! What are some ways in which our earth, and all creation, is programmed to be on "automatic recycling"?

Delight

November 5, 2010

Delight! One of my favorite words, for sure. Even on the worst of days there's always so much in which to delight. Today was filled with delights: the sun finally came out after two days of soggy, dreary weather, and friends came to discuss our Pet & Heroes event--and brought a birthday cake and Christmas cactus to celebrate my upcoming birthday. I also swam at the health club (the one day when the swim teams don't monopolize the pool) and had a doubly delightful walk with Jessie—marveling at her joyful trot *and* what's left of the gorgeous fall foliage.

What else do I delight in? A wonderful husband and a daughter who's at a good place in her life—and an adorable little granddaughter, at just the right age to remind us of what a miracle life really is! I also delight in our new pastor and his wonderful wife, and the way our church is growing in God's direction, and the list goes on and on… The Psalmist says, *This is the day the Lord has made. Let us rejoice and be glad in it!* *(118:24),* which is another way of saying "Delight in what God has given us *today*"—and that's just what I plan to do.

Let's take another perspective and ask "What can we do to delight the Lord?" Samuel tells the Israelites (in 1 Samuel 15:22) that what delights God is not our religious actions (such as sacrificing animals, which was done at that time), but our willingness to listen and obey. In order to do that we have to spend time reaching out to God and getting to know what it is he wants of us. The prophet Micah pinpointed it by saying: *What does the Lord require of you but to do justly, to love mercy, and to walk humbly with your God? (Micah 6:8)* A great life-long challenge.

Ps 37:4 is fantastic: "Delight in the Lord and he will give you the desires
of your heart." A double blessing! The inexplicable joy of delighting
in our awesome God and being blessed with dreams come true.

It's stewardship time at our church, time to pledge our monetary support.
We're to give joyfully and gratefully—not grudgingly, out of guilt.
Pastor Chuck says that we grow our faith with this type of giving.

Shall I increase my pledge despite our spending more than we're earning?
I think it's time to step out in faith and do more than suggested.
I hope it delights you, Lord, as much as it does me!

What About You?

1. I delight in enjoying people, especially children, because one of the
    best gifts I can give to others is to thoroughly enjoy them. In what do
    you take delight?

2. Jesus said he came to give us the abundant life—a life in which we
    find many delights. How can knowing and loving Jesus bring us life's
    greatest delights?

3. What Biblical stories, promises, and Scriptures delight you the most?

Sponsor

November 11, 2010

When we were first married and living in New York City, my "agnostic" husband insisted that we go to Norman Vincent Peale's church on West 29th Street. Dr. Peale's book, "The Power of Positive Thinking," was (and still is) a classic, translated into many languages. Hugo's mom in Switzerland even had a copy in German. Dr. Peale was fantastic, and soon I decided to join his church. In order to help us newcomers feel at home and learn the ropes (e.g. how to sneak ahead of the hundreds of visitors waiting in line each Sunday) we were assigned sponsors. Al and Anne were our sponsors. We met over a light meal at a nearby restaurant and became lifelong friends. Some 40+ years later we still keep in touch, even though neither we nor they have attended Marble Collegiate Church in many years. We moved to New Jersey, but continued attending Marble to hear Dr. Peale's amazing "no notes" sermons...until our daughter was born. We brought her to Dr. Peale to be baptized, but eventually found a nearby church—about the same time he retired.

Over the years I have thoroughly enjoyed being on the other end of the sponsorship, too. As a young, unmarried woman I volunteered with a group that matched troubled teens with mentors. Linda and I kept in touch for many years—hmmm, wonder what she's doing now... I also "adopted" a needy child through Christian Children's Fund (now called ChildWorld), paying a monthly sponsorship amount and writing back and forth on occasion. I can't believe that I'm still (almost 45 years later) doing this. I'm now sponsoring my 5th or 6th child, one unbroken line of wonderful youngsters who all too quickly, but thankfully, became capable adults, able to lead productive lives in their native India.

264

Our foundation, Open Doors, enjoys sponsoring events and causes that help both people and animals. It's such fun to make purchases and donations to benefit deserving people and organizations.

Helping long distance is nice, but being on the front line is really special. It's more fun--and more challenging—to reach out and be face to face with people and situations in need of a loving touch.

I've been a one-on-one friend and mentor—and friend to a whole houseful of girls waiting to be adopted or returned to their families. The rewards are priceless even though not all of my efforts have succeeded.

What About You?

1. When have you been the "sponsor" (helping another in a caring and helpful manner)? When have you been on the receiving end?

2. What are some ways in which we can be sponsors and ambassadors for God?

3. The prophet Elijah mentored his assistant Elisha, and Elisha ended up getting double the power Elijah had. Jesus molded his disciples and promised that they would do even greater things than he had (Jn 14:12). How can we empower others in a similar fashion so they, too, will "outshine" us?

Steady

November 14, 2010

We steady something when it's crooked or shaky. Like our nerves, when they get out of control. In Aesop's well-known fable, the tortoise was steady. He kept his eyes on the finish line and never stopped moving toward it... Remember? Slow and steady wins the race! Falling right in with today's theme are two people discussed at Bible Study and church today: William Wilberforce and Sarah Hale. Both were steadfast in their convictions and actions, trying again and again, year after year, until they succeeded—Wilberforce in stopping the slave trade to Great Britain and Hale in getting Thanksgiving recognized as a national holiday.

St. Paul was steadfast: first, in becoming a Pharisee, then in persecuting the Christians, and finally to spreading the Gospel to as many people as possible. God wants us to stay on a steady keel as we face the storms of life. Isaiah gives us a hint on how to do that in the Book which bears his name (26:3): *Thou wilt keep him in perfect peace, whose mind is stayed on thee: because he trusteth in thee.*

I've been steady on some things—loving my husband of 43 years and sharing my faith with him while waiting for God to grant him child-like faith, supporting needy children in India through a monthly donation and letters, and studying the Bible for years (which continues to this day). I regret, however, having given up on other things—such as making an annual anniversary card describing each year together (given up long ago). How I'd love to have those years documented with stories and pictures, the way I started doing it years ago.

Let's be constant in our love and respect for God, ourselves, and others.
With our feet on the solid Rock (Jesus) we'll make rough places straight,
remain calm amid chaos, take the bigger view, and hold our ground.

I have felt your steadying hand, Lord, enabling me to forget myself and
find latent goodness and talent within. Thanks for helping me
through tough times and giving me a husband with equanimity.

You've increased my faith and emotional stability through others' examples.
Today's word tells me it's time for me to steady others. Even though
I'm still balancing my own life I know I can help others in many ways.

What About You?

1. When have others (and God) helped to balance and steady you?

2. How can we help others gain a sense of well-being and build their lives on God's rock-solid promises?

3. Jesus kept in contact with his Father and used Scripture (Mt 4:1-11) to help him stay true to his mission. How did he steady others, and reward others' steadfastness when he saw it?

267

Conduct

November 16, 2010

This past week I received an email from a friend—a musical friend I've known since kindergarten. Donna is one of those rare people with "perfect pitch." She can tell us that the telephone is ringing on a B-flat or we're slightly off pitch. She sent me an Internet video of a little 3-year-old conducting a fantastic Beethoven piece—lengthy, diverse, and awe-inspiring. Well, this little guy is a natural—he knew every little innuendo and loved every moment of his heartfelt directing. As the piece worked its way to the final climax he was filled with such verve and gusto that the baton flew right out of his hand—and he ended up laughing and rolling around in delight to the final bars of Beethoven's dramatic piece.

Donna said she sent me this because it reminded her of our high school band, when we played great classical works like this one. God has a way of taking our memories and using them to spur us on to new awareness and new opportunities. I now fondly recall my time in the band, and also find some interesting lessons in the actions of this little maestro:

* Let your heart and passion play a large part in choosing how you will conduct your life.
* Lose yourself in giving your all to whatever it is you are doing. (See Colossians 3:23)
* If things go wrong, roll with the punches and even enjoy it if you can!

Most of all, we need to remember *whose* we are, and conduct ourselves accordingly. We are God's ambassadors here on earth. We want others to see *him*, through *us*.

Music has played a big part in my life, although I'm not especially gifted.
Just loving to sing and loving the Lord led me to conduct the children's
choir for 17 years. Sometimes our hearts outshine our talents!

Now I conduct sing-along groups with developmentally-challenged adults
and Alzheimer patients. Just this week we got both groups together
for a delightful musical gathering. Jessie the dog joined us.

Life is fun when we conduct ourselves in a way that makes life fun for
others, too. "Enthusiasm Makes the Difference," said Dr. Peale.
Here I am, Lord—ready to do whatever conducting you have in mind.

What About You?

1. Are you pleased with the way in which you are conducting your life? How are you enjoying life and making it fun for others, too?

2. How do you think God might be calling you to conduct something new or to conduct something differently?

3. What can we learn from the way Jesus conducted his life, death, resurrection? How do other people (Biblical or otherwise) inspire us to make changes, do more, and expand our horizons?

Salute

November 20, 2010

Salute, of course, refers to that formal gesture of respect (hand to forehead or heart) for/by service personnel or when pledging allegiance to our flag. But, as we ponder today's word, let's look at its broader meanings, which include giving others well-deserved attention in the form of greetings, praises, and acknowledgments.

Last November our non-profit organization, Open Doors, had its first *Salute to Pets and Heroes* to celebrate our pets and honor those on the front line of animal rescue in our area. It was a wonderful event, but not enough people attended. Our second annual salute will be at a different time of the year, on a different day of the week and time of day, at a different venue--and will spotlight new key guests in the hopes of attracting more people. Maybe I'll even get to share my lighthearted poem, "Owed to Our Pets" that I wasn't able to read last time.

It's always good to think about those to whom we'd like to say "Hats off to you"...for being helpful, thoughtful, courageous, a good example, etc. And we can do that as we go about our everyday lives, in natural, less formal ways. In fact, we can make it a habit to recognize people and accomplishments that deserve a word of thanks or a pat on the back. Another good habit is stressing the good about people when we speak to others about them. I salute those who do that on a regular basis!

270

I salute those martyrs who spread the Good News, translated the Bible, and spread God's love throughout the world. I also salute those whose inventions make our lives so much better—may we use their contributions wisely.

I salute those who sacrifice comfort and safety to protect/help us and others…those who take unpopular stands for righteous reasons, bring good out of evil, and give their all for our benefit and God's glory.

My husband, Hugo, excels in encouraging, listening, and complimenting me on my efforts. How can I do the same for him, Lord? Thanks for increasing my wisdom, discernment, understanding, humility, and compassion so I can grow gratefully and happily in your direction!

What About You?

1. Whom do you salute, have you saluted, and should you salute—and why?

2. When and why have you been saluted by others?

3. How can we honor God and thank him for who he is, what he's done, and what he promises?

Rise

November 21, 2010

Rise and shine and give God the glory! That's great advice for the start of each and every day. There's nothing like the pre-dawn hours for getting in touch with our Maker. Jesus was an early riser, and used those first hours to be with our Father, too. (E.g., Mark 1:35).

As a pre-teen at Methodist summer camp, the "Morning Watch" was well worth the early rising. I still recall the joy I felt as I took in the early morning sights and smells…just me, my Bible, and my Lord. And sunrise service at the Grand Canyon was an experience I'll never forget. Just this morning I thanked Hugo for encouraging me, so many years later, to get up earlier than I normally would. It's hard for me (I enjoy lavishing in bed) but it's by far the best way to start the day. Hugo has early rising down to an art. He's even written a booklet and some e-books about waking up with abundant energy—and sustaining it throughout the day. He also teaches classes on the subject. And best of all, at 81 years of age, he practices what he preaches.

The word *rise* also makes me think of *rising to the occasion*. We don't know what the future will bring our way, but when we spend the time and effort to draw as close as we can to the Lord we are well equipped to handle the surprises and challenges of life. I just received an email announcing that Ron, a longtime church member and friend, died today. We had a special bond with him after our church's trip to the Holy Land in the nineties. Hugo and I both agreed that he was a wonderfully amazing person. Hugo, my resident "agnostic," then said: "What good did it do him? He died anyway." My response? "The difference comes in what happens *after* death!"

Ron and his wife, Sue (both widowed earlier), loved being together. They "gave back" by hosting meetings for people overcome with grief. Ron's death is a big loss, but Sue will rise above it with God's help.

I think of William Merrill's hymn, Rise Up, O Men of God! (Women, too!) And I think of Jesus, rising from death and giving us a glimpse into what God has in store for us as we take up our cross and follow him.

The women who rose early and went to the tomb were first to learn that Jesus had indeed risen. One of the women, Mary, was first to see him alive again. Now we can all we rise up and call him Savior.

What About You?

1. When did you rise to a difficult challenge? How have you helped others and/or others helped you to do the same? How has God helped us?

2. What Biblical people, stories, or passages come to mind when you think of the word *rise*?

3. What are some ways in which we can rise and shine for the Lord?

Cooperate

November 23, 2010

If the weather cooperates I'll soon be out with Jessie for our morning walk. If it doesn't cooperate we'll still walk, but with a doggy raincoat for Jessie and an umbrella for me. Then we'll cooperate with each other for another relaxing, enjoyable jaunt. I generally let Jessie "call the shots" as to where we'll go and at what pace—I enjoy watching her trot happily ahead of me and make the decisions as to which turns we'll take. It makes every walk unique and fun.

Life is so wonderfully pleasant when we cooperate, so I say "Amen!" to our word for today. No wonder the Epistles are filled with commands to get along and, as much as possible, to be at peace with one another. And no wonder Jesus praises the peacemakers. The world, so full of dissension, sorely needs every bit of mellowing we can possibly bring to it. Jesus calls us to be the both light and salt, making things better and more pleasant for all—those we know and those we'll never know on this side of Heaven.

Hugo and I "agree to disagree" in a congenial way. That gives us the freedom to express ourselves honestly and openly, so that a respectful dialog can ensue—to draw us closer together rather than farther apart. We've had our ups and downs communicating with our daughter during her growing years, but now we get along beautifully. Sadly, I've seen people "write others off" without making an effort to understand others' views or actions—or even attempt to explain their own. I've also done this and, looking back, I wish I'd been kinder and more cooperative—gentler with people's feelings, more genuine and sincere. Thankfully, it's never too late to do better.

Thank heaven for a God of love, compassion, and forgiveness.
What a great model for us! With God's help I'm ready to
cooperate with scary, inevitable things: change, aging, grief, death...

Grant me an extra dose of grace, dear Lord, so I'll be more cooperative
with others when I'd rather make some unnecessary waves.
Like St. Francis, I'll sow good things when and where they're needed.

Ps 139 says: "Search me, O Lord, and know my heart; test me and know
my anxious thoughts. See if there is any offensive way in me; and lead
me in the way everlasting." I yield to your findings and leadership, Lord.

What About You?

1. When have you cooperated (or failed to do so) in the past? What do you learn from those experiences? When might cooperation *not* be possible—and WWJD (what would Jesus do) in those instances?

2. The wisdom of Solomon tells us that if one person falls another can help, and a triple-braided cord isn't easily broken. What are some other examples of the power of cooperation?

3. What can you and I do right now in response to Jill Jackson Miller's 1955 song "Let There Be Peace on Earth" (and let it begin with me)?

Benefit

November 26, 2010

The more we think about it the more we realize that we're benefiting in countless and amazing ways from others' inventiveness and hard work. I'd hate to give up our garage door opener, my gas fireplace on a cold morning, or (God forbid!) my washer/dryer. Hugo clings to his small radio, his computer, and our car. And we're both extremely grateful to those who devised our toileting and heating/cooling systems—and the airplane that will soon take us on vacation.

Let's also consider how we've benefited from friendships with others—and they, with us. And, most of *all*, how we all benefit from God's love in our lives. God's gifts are the most important of all things beneficial; it's to our detriment that we ignore or misuse them. Jesus asks: *What will you gain if you own the whole world, but destroy yourself or waste your life? (Lk 9:25)*

Today's word inspires us to be a benefit to others as we enjoy the many benefits in our own lives. Tonight was one of those mutually beneficial evenings. Our friend, Steve (president of the local theater group) again gave a group of us permission to attend the dress rehearsal of the annual children's musical. This year it's a wonderful show entitled "Honk" (a take off on the ugly duckling story that carries wonderful life lessons). It's a doubly fun-filled production because it has several children acting in it—as ducklings. Our group consisted of little ones, ages 6 through 12, from a nearby Children's Aid group home, and several friends of all ages who love being with the little girls who are spending the holidays away from their families. After the show our charitable foundation, Open Doors, treated to hot chocolate at Cool Beans, a nearby coffee shop.

*Thank you, Lord, for all our benefits. May we recognize and enjoy them—
and do all we can to help others do the same. Without you, our lives
would be barren. All thanks, praise, and glory be yours forever! Amen*

*A nonagenarian in our church, Sally, knows many Psalms by heart. One of her
favorites is 103, which starts this way: "Bless the Lord, O my soul, and
forget not his benefits" and goes on to delineate what they are.*

*And now, Lord, I ask: "What I can do to be a better steward of your many
blessings? What changes can I implement to benefit you and others?" The
more I ask these questions and live the answers, the more **I** benefit.*

What About You?

1.   What modern-day and God-given benefits (as in Ps 103) do you most
     enjoy/appreciate/treasure?

2.   How can we, and others, benefit from a closer relationship with God/
     Jesus/Holy Spirit?

3.   What are some ways in which we can gain from this Word-a-Day
     discipline?

Deny

November 28, 2010

Like so many other words, *deny* is a doubled-edged sword. Peter denied Jesus, claiming he never knew him—just minutes after bragging that he would follow Him to the death. And I suspect that the unpardonable sin is to deny the truth, calling it evil and then calling evil good.

The other, more positive edge to *deny* is when we deny our children (and ourselves) things that are unnecessary or harmful—to build character and/or pass along values. In Matthew 16:24 Jesus says to deny ourselves, pick up our crosses, and follow him. The modern translations replace the word *deny* with: *putting aside selfish ambition* (New Living Translation), *forgetting about ourselves* (Contemporary English Version), and *saying no to what we want* (Easy-to-Read Version). This type of denial generally benefits us and any others who are touched by it.

Just yesterday I read a story in Guideposts about Ann Curry, the news anchor for the Today show. Her father, a career Navy man, taught her and her siblings never to say, "It's not fair," because whining accomplishes nothing. So when Ann was denied her wish to replace Katie Couric as co-host of *Today*, she asked herself "What is it I *need* to be doing?" She then recognized her deep-seated passion to do humanitarian reporting: finding people suffering far from the eyes of the world and getting their stories out, making people care about them. Says Ann: *Journalism should do more then inform. It should make you care.* Though her travels take time away from her family, she continues to do God's work in Iraq, Afghanistan, Iran, Pakistan, India, the Congo, and Darfur—so far.

*Help me, Lord, to never deny Jesus by what I say or do. In Mark 8:38
Jesus says: Don't be ashamed of me and my message…[or] the Son of Man
will be ashamed of you when he comes in the glory of his Father…*

*Help me, Lord, to never deny the truth. In John 8:31-2 Jesus said: "If you
keep obeying…You will know the truth, and the truth will set you free."
Freedom in Christ strengthens our honesty, integrity, kindness…*

*so I can deny myself and let go of self-indulgent, unhealthy living.
I can slay my "demons" with the sword of the Spirit (Eph 6:10-8).
I can recognize evil and deny it any access to my Christ-filled life.*

What About You?

1. When have *you* denied the truth by telling little "white" (or not so
    white) lies? How did it affect your relationship with God and others?
    How can it be "made right?"

2. When have you denied yourself something? What was the outcome?

3. What does it mean to pick up our crosses and follow Jesus? How
    can we do that right now? Who do you consider to be good role
    models for this?

Know

November 29, 2010

When we think about all the things there are to know in this world, it's mind-boggling—and the facts keep multiplying as I write this. Amid the maze of ever-changing data, both accurate and inaccurate, it's comforting to know that *All I Really Need to Know I Learned in Kindergarten* (book by Robert Fulghum). Among the examples he cites are sharing, playing fairly, not hitting others, putting things back, not taking what isn't ours, and saying we're sorry when we do wrong. My favorite is: *When you go out into the world, watch for traffic, hold hands, and stick together.*

My computer savvy ends with email. I have a very limited knowledge of iPods, blackberries, Facebook, and twittering. But what I'm able to do with my faithful Apple iMac is amazing. It has enabled me to be much more prolific while improving the quality of my writing. I can Google almost anything and learn all I need to know in a matter of minutes (How else do you think I was just able to describe Mr. Fulghum's book and spout some its contents--and even spell his name correctly?) It makes my work so much more enjoyable and gratifying.

What's even more rewarding is what I would call a *spiritual knowing*. It's being able to recognize and implement what really matters. St. Paul says (in 1 Co 13:1-3) that even if we speak all languages, understand all secrets and knowledge, give away everything, and have a deep faith, it's meaningless (we *are* nothing and *gain* nothing) unless we love others. It's a knowing that God is God, the center of our joy and giver of an inner peace that passes human understanding. *Be still and know that I am God,* says the Psalmist. (46:10)

Amid his suffering, Job says (19:23-9): "I know that my Redeemer lives!
And at the end he'll stand on this earth. My flesh may be destroyed,
yet from this body I will see God for myself." I long for that moment.

A hymn by Ira Stamphill talks about the importance of Who we know:
"Many things about tomorrow I don't seem to understand, but
I know who holds the future and I know who holds my hand."

Peter was the first to call Jesus the Messiah, and Thomas was first to
call him "my Lord and my God," acknowledging that Jesus is God.
Show us the way, Lord, so we, too, can be faithful and knowledgeable.

What About You?

1. What knowledge do *you* have that you (others and/or God) deem
    to be especially valuable?

2. What or whom would you like to know or know *better*? What can you
    do to help that to happen?

3. God blessed us with brains and it's our job to keep them active and
    constantly absorbing new knowledge to use in helpful, productive
    ways. What ideas come to mind?

Arrive

December 4, 2010

When we left New Jersey yesterday we pondered the word *leave,* so it's logical that today's word would be *arrive.* We arrived in two Florida locations—first in West Palm Beach where we got the royal treatment (picked up by Danny, Elisa and 14-month old granddaughter Jessica). We ate out for lunch and they loaned us a car so we wouldn't have to rent one; then we headed for our annual 2-week vacation in Sanibel. And when we arrived *here* we were greeted with lemonade and cookies at the front desk. What a great start it was to our fourteen days in this tropical paradise: a view of the Gulf of Mexico from our second-floor unit, palm trees and other non-New Jersey foliage...but weather a little colder than expected. (Nothing's perfect!) The great thing is that we'll get to see friends and family here in Florida—loved ones we'd never get to see otherwise.

When we think in terms of our entire life journeys, we realize that we never fully "arrive." We're always pushing forward—and even if we want to stop the movement of time or wrap ourselves in a cocoon and say, "Stop the world; I want to get off!" it's futile. Like it or not, we're either moving purposefully toward something or fighting against the inevitable (like trying to stand still while hurricane-strength winds blow all around us, moving us along with it anyway.)

Graciously, God doesn't reveal the future to us. How can we enjoy the present if we're able to see what lies ahead of us? God mercifully designed us so we can enjoy the moment we're in. And, in addition, he blesses us daily with small "arrivals" to make our journeys interesting and enjoyable...

Babies arrive, company comes, we gain an insight or see a gorgeous sunset.
These little arrivals are God's gifts to us as we move toward our great
"arrival" into his Kingdom—an arrival that defies the tooth of time.

This is Advent, when we symbolically await the arrival of Baby Jesus.
What a priceless gift Jesus is—the greatest Gift of all,
arriving for everyone and anyone who welcomes him.

And we're promised a second arrival, when Jesus will return again.
All will be changed for the better and Isaiah's description of a
truly peaceful earth (11:1-10) will have arrived—and us, too!

What About You?

1. What small (and not-so-small) "arrivals" in *your* life are now happy (or not-so-happy) memories? How do you feel about them now? How can you extract some good from the not-so-happy ones?

2. What pulls you forward in life? What are you "eyeing" as your final destination?

3. Has Jesus arrived in your life? How might you introduce him to others?

Congregate

December 5, 2010

Here's a word that should come easy to me—I've been active in the Congregational Church for decades. And even here in Sanibel we attend a Congregational UCC (United Church of Christ) church. In fact, we went there today and got to "congregate" with our dear friends, Andy and Gladdy, from Ohio. They come to Sanibel for the same three weeks each year, which overlap with our two weeks. Then, after church and a look in at the church's "Unique Boutique" sale, we enjoyed a nice lunch with our Midwestern friends.

In addition, we got to see (and hear) our favorite pastor, John Danner, who's now senior pastor here in Sanibel. As always, he had an interesting and inspiring message to share. And at the boutique we ran into his wonderful wife, Linda. We'll "congregate" with them over lunch later in the week!

Also today, I spoke with loved ones whom we get to see just once a year when we're here in Sanibel: sister-in-law Larraine (from Marco Island, FL) and sister Janet (from Bradenton, FL). We'll gather with them next Sunday, which would be our mom's 100th birthday. In her honor we decided to make it a very big gathering right here at our Casa Ybel resort. We'll have my brother and wife, sister and hubby, niece and four children, Elisa/Danny/granddaughter Jessica, and Danny's "mom" (who raised him from age nine). Add Hugo, me, and our Mid-western friends and we'll total 17 (I think). And I'll also invite my niece's husband (18). Hope the weather works with us so we can be outside by the pools and enjoy the Gulf with its resort activities.

What a joy it is to congregate with those who love the Lord—and us, too!
Jesus said he'd be with two or three gathered in his name (Mt 18:20).
May all our gatherings honor you, Lord Jesus, both in church and out.

Today Pastor Danner spoke about peace and the peaceful spirit that can be
exercised when we're frustrated--like when we're at a crowded
airport or when a telemarketer interrupts our dinner.

All of us on planet earth are fellow congregants, sharing the earth
and being loved by a forgiving God. Let's pray for peace, and
live it as best we can this holiday season and always.

What About You?

1. What are some examples of people getting together for good (and perhaps not-so-good) purposes?

2. What gatherings stand out in your memory as particularly special? Why?

3. How can you be a positive influence on those with whom you congregate?

Influence

December 7, 2010

Are you a person of influence? Our former pastor, John Danner (whom we'll be meeting for lunch tomorrow) once told me that I wield more power than I realize. And looking back at my early years as lieutenant of our elementary school's safety patrol, babysitter, and playground director—and my later roles as a third-grade teacher, vacation Bible school teacher, director of kids' choirs, and writer of the local Girl Scout newsletter—I tend to agree. I have certainly had the good fortune of living in the right place at the right time. I recall when women had trouble getting credit cards, and church ushers, deacons and pastors were all men. Now women do everything.

Hugo and I have always been very much equal partners. He's a Swiss who was way ahead of his time. When we married, Swiss women couldn't yet vote in his motherland, yet he pushed me "forward and up" in every way he could. I credit him for getting me into writing. Because of his encouragement and influence, I applied for (and received) a sabbatical leave from teaching, one year at half pay, to write an educational book. I got pregnant at the same time, so it took me longer than expected to write the book, but I stuck with it and my book about the Secrets of A+ Teaching (published by Parker Publishing) greatly increased my love of writing. Hugo's editing assistance honed my writing skills and greatly influenced the tenor and quality of my writing.

Other great influencers in my life were my parents, Howard and Grace Olnowich, and my brother and sister (Howard and Janet). Relatives, friends, and boyfriends have left major imprints, too. I sometimes still dream of Dave, a longtime pre-teen and teen boyfriend.

286

*An English teacher, a Latin teacher, and band directors also come to mind.
And I sometimes think about a childhood classmate whose enthusiasm
and friendliness inspire me to be more like him.*

*Pastors at Methodist summer camp, Young Life leader (Harv), and of course
Billy Graham, the great evangelist, all influenced my spiritual growth.
And you, Father-Son-and-Spirit, have influenced me the most!*

*May our charitable trust, Open Doors, influence many lives, especially
those in need of a relationship with you. Forgive the times I
missed/misused an opportunity, and send me forth as a good influence.*

What About You?

1. Who has changed *your* life for the better over the years? What bad
    influences do you also recall? How have *you* influenced others,
    positively and perhaps not-so-positively?

2. What are some memorable examples of how God and/or Jesus
    influenced people (from the Bible or from your life experience)?

3. Who would you most like to influence right now? Why? How might
    you do that?

Zip

December 8, 2010

Zip-a-dee-doo-dah! Thanks, Lord, for this happy song that brings back so many happy memories. It comes from a Disney movie, "Song of the South," which I saw more than sixty years ago. It was my first big-screen movie. I loved this song then and still do. I sing it with my nursing home friends as well as the little girls in the pre-adoptive group home.

Of course the word *zip* brings other thoughts to mind as well—the zipper, for instance. It's a clever invention that got its start way back in 1851 and made its way, through a series of innovations, to become a highly preferred closure in today's world. Hugo and I much prefer a sweater or jacket with a zipper as opposed to a number of buttons. There's something no-nonsense and yet cozy about zipping up.

Now, zipping up our mouths is another thing entirely. That's something I still need to work on. The thought that every word we utter is still floating around in the atmosphere is a frightening thought—as is the thought that one day we'll have to account to God for all the words we speak. Mark 4:22 tells us that everything hidden will be made public and all secrets will be well known. So the more we zip up our mouths, the better. I certainly regret countless words I've spoken in anger, ignorance, thoughtlessness, and outright meanness.

We also have to zip up our pants and be like our spiritual forebears. The early Christian church had just a few simple rules, and one was to stay clear of sexual immorality. (Acts 15:29)

In my lifespan I've seen our morals take a downward slide. The misuse of God's great gift of sexuality causes untold pain. Heavy on my heart are innocents being abused, human trafficking, mutilated females, etc.

Zip also means to rush, such as the way I zip through the newspaper, etc. I hurry, I multi-task, I lose patience, and I still arrive late. A psychologist once called me "driven." Ouch! Help me, Lord!

I don't want to be "driven" and zip through life. Today in Florida we attended an Advent Bible study, then enjoyed lunch with our former pastor and his wife. Help me to savor life and be driven only by love.

What About You?

1. What happy song(s) and other blessings make it a zip-a-dee-doo-dah day for you?

2. When have you later wished you'd kept your mouth or pants zipped up? When have you taken your regrets to the Lord and asked for forgiveness and guidance going forward?

3. Must of us zip through life without savoring God's Word. How can we change that?

Exceed

December 9, 2010

Here we are in Sanibel, Florida—a place that exceeds most people's expectations. It's an island paradise with picturesque views and a peaceful ambiance. It's a great place for people who love nature and consider the sunset the best show in town. And it's a great place for collecting shells because many different kinds wash up onto its beaches daily. And from the middle of the island one can see both the sunrise and the sunset because the island bends like a boomerang.

We first came to Sanibel more than forty years ago and loved it. Hugo later showed it to a Swiss friend who wanted to buy property to vacation in the US—and for twelve years we enjoyed his lovely home on the Gulf. We missed Sanibel when our friend sold his property, so we bought a couple of timeshare weeks in order to keep coming. We always have the same weeks in December, and even when the weather disappoints us (as it has thus far this time, with its record cold) we still find lots of things that exceed our expectations. Just today we ate at "Sweet Tomatoes"—and it was so good that its *exceed* became our *excess*! The same happens at Golden Corral, our favorite buffet, which is prevalent in Florida but quite scarce in New Jersey (which is good for our waistlines!).

Sanibel's new recreation center also exceeded our expectations today. For a modest fee, we timeshare owners (mini-taxpayers) get the use of a fantastic exercise room, outdoor swimming pools, and a wide variety of classes. We signed up for a week and started with our first workout today. We definitely have to work off the eating excesses mentioned above! I'd also like to try their yoga class because I did some yoga years ago and enjoyed it.

290

*You always exceed my expectations, Lord. Whenever we team up on
a project I'm never disappointed—instead, I'm amazed at the results.
I know I shouldn't be surprised, but I always am.*

*How can I exceed my goals and expectations, Lord, and get closer to yours?
I can think bigger, and with your help, I can grow into the purposes you
have for me—over and above, outside the box, and through the barriers!*

*Jesus tells of peace that surpasses understanding, going the extra mile,
and sowing seed that multiplies a hundredfold. Paul says we can't begin
to imagine what God has in store for those who love him (1 Co 2:9).*

What About You?

1. When have your expectations been exceeded?

2. What Biblical, historical, and/or personal examples show how God
    can far exceed people's expectations?

3. Are there any not-so-good excesses in *your* life that need attending to?
    What good things can you do to exceed your (and others')
    expectations?

Turn

December 14, 2010

John the Baptist (forerunner to Jesus) and Jesus himself had similar messages. John's was: *Turn back to God and be baptized. (Mk 1:4)* Jesus' was: *The time has come. God's kingdom will soon be here. Turn back to God and believe the Good News. (Mk 1:15)* We all have some turning to do in order to be in right relationship with our maker and our savior. Sometimes we even have to turn away from those closest to us. Jesus said his message would separate even close family members. (Mt 10:35) My marrying an agnostic has resulted in a crevice between Hugo and me, but with God's help we've been able to bridge it. Joel Osteen's message today was about God's timing. God sets a time for the realization of our dreams, prayers, goals, etc. We just have to be patient and wait for God's timing. So I'll keep praying for Hugo's leap of faith.

How grateful I am that our daughter and family have turned to God and are constantly growing in his direction. And I hope and pray that all of my projects (present and future) will turn people's thoughts and hearts in God's direction. The year 2010 is almost finished—as is this Word-a-Day discipline. In 2011, Lord willing, I will write (along with my dog, Jessie) a sequel to her first book, *Bark Up the Right Tree, Lessons from a Rescued Dog.* We hope to make it as inspiring and faith-filled as the first one was.

I anticipate some turns in the road ahead. At our ages (67 and 81) we see more and more people pass on. Two close friends are already widows, loved ones face health problems—even Hugo has a cataract operation coming up.

*We have big decisions to make this decade: where to live, how to use time
and money, etc. And when it's our turn to face the inevitable, we'll
lean on you, Lord, for the grace and strength to handle it well.*

*Jesus turned water into wine, making the ordinary something extraordinary.
Watching a little one explore the world to learn new things makes the
the ordinary extraordinary, too--for doting parents and grandparents.*

*We're enjoying our little 14-month-old Jessica so much! I pray that we,
her family, can turn her in a direction that will bring pride and
joy, not just to her parents and us, but to our Heavenly Father, too.*

What About You?

1. Jesus tells us to turn the other cheek and gives some examples in Mt 5:38-42. How can an attitude like this turn things around for all concerned, and how can we apply this in our everyday lives today?

2. The songs "Turn, Turn" and "Sunrise, Sunset" remind us that seasons come and go. How can turning to God help us handle change?

3. "Tis the Gift" is a Shaker melody that talks about bowing, bending, and turning...until we turn out right! What is "right" for you?

Champion

December 16, 2010

Being a champion doesn't appeal to me so much, but being able to champion a cause or a person sounds great! I can already champion and encourage our little granddaughter, Jessica, by giving her priceless gifts (such as enjoying her, believing in her, giving of my time and attention, etc.). No one needs to be idle or feel useless, because there are so many reasons and ways to champion the good in life and in people.

As we age, Hugo and I are tending to champion warm, sunny weather—more and more. We're glad that our daughter, Elisa, has settled into a warmer (rather than a colder) clime. While here in Sanibel we've checked out the rental situations in the hopes of coming back down for at least two consecutive months next winter. We've had a cold two weeks here this time, but today is getting milder again—up in the 70s. Tomorrow will be even nicer—just when we'll be returning to New Jersey!

My greatest desire is to champion Jesus, God's Kingdom, the Bible, and the church. I look forward to using my booklet, *Following Jesus Today and Every Day* and this Word-a-Day book to help me do just that. The little class I taught on happiness ("Happy and Free, a Change in Me") went well; perhaps I can do that again in some fashion. My greatest "vehicle" for championing the Lord is our non-profit foundation, Open Doors, which has already championed a lot of good ideas and events—and, with God's help, the best is yet to come!

In so many ways you have championed me, Lord. A loving family prayed for me before I was even born. Ps 139 expresses my sentiments exactly: "You have laid your hand upon me…your works are wonderful…"

Jesus championed the overlooked and abused. He championed those who trusted and believed in him, obeyed him, and needed him. He especially champions those who spread his Good News.

May I always seek "champion the verb" rather than the noun. A true champion champions others and God—in ways that bring out the most, the best, the truest, the healthiest, and the most wonderful of all!

What About You?

1. Who have you championed, and who has championed you? How does God champion us?

2. What causes are most in need of support these days? How can we help?

3. The Bible says (Mt 6:21) that our treasure is where our heart is; in essence, we champion what we focus on. How should we change our focus today—as individuals, communities, a world?

Exemplify

December 18, 2010

It's nice to be back home from our two weeks in Florida. Despite the cold, wintry weather there's no place like home! As 2010 draws to a close I start thinking (as usual) about the upcoming year and how I can live a better life and stay better focused on my goal, mission and purpose in life: to draw closer to God, to bring others closer, to do all for God's glory.

Today's word, *exemplify*, reminds me that I must *be* a living example of what I profess. I must "walk the talk" that comes out of my mouth. What angered Jesus the most were the "religious" people of his day. They knew the Scriptures inside and out, tithed their money and possessions, and claimed all the honors due to them...yet they cheated widows, misused their power, and led people astray. Jesus called them hypocrites, saying: *You are like whitewashed tombs which on the outside appear beautiful, but inside they are full of dead men's bones and all uncleanness.* (Matthew 23:27)

I'd like to be a *do-as-I-do-without-my-saying-anything* type of person—one who inspires others to take the high road without preaching. I think back to so many times when I made things worse and alienated people by saying too much and/or saying the wrong things. Looking ahead, I'd like to be a quiet doer who concentrates on serving God and loving others (and vice versa). So, I'm adding a new book to my morning devotional time, replacing Billy Graham's "Journey" (finally finished) with Dr. Harold C. Cutler and the Dalai Lama's handbook for living, *The Art of Happiness*. This will be a nice addition to the Biblical Scriptures that are my mainstay.

I'm also adding a book called "Smart Organizing," which I left in Florida and had mailed back to me. It helps me to get my house in order, and I already see that it can help me keep my life in order, too.

When I consider the best examples in my own life, I think of my Aunt Florence (my grandma's cousin, Flossie) who exemplified enthusiasm and generosity, and my dad: patience and determination.

Hugo exemplifies diligence/fidelity; my daughter and sister: common sense. My mom: kindness and trust in God. Billy Graham: confidence and faith; my dog, Jessie: devotion; and my Savior: love and compassion.

What About You?

1. Who have been good examples in *your* life?

2. What sort of an example have *you* been and/or would like to be?

3. When has a bad example inspired you (or others) to go in the opposite direction?

Resist

Now that the new year is quickly approaching I think about all the things I should resolve to resist in the coming year—like the urge to eat unhealthy food, the tendency to complain, procrastinating, letting the unimportant sidetrack me from the important, worrying about how I look, spending too much money, wasting time, saying the foolish thing... and the list goes on and on. Maybe I'd do well to resist approaching things from a negative perspective, and take a more pro-active, positive approach.

Instead of centering my resolutions around what I don't want to do, I might follow the advice of the Dalai Lama (head of state and spiritual leader in Tibet). In the book, *The Art of Happiness*, Howard C. Cutler, MD, quotes him as saying: *Will it bring me happiness? That simple question can be a powerful tool in helping us skillfully conduct all areas of our lives, not just in the decision to indulge in drugs or that third piece of banana cream pie. It...shifts the focus from what we are denying ourselves to what we are seeking. (p. 36)*

Happiness, as described by the Dalai Lama, is stable and persistent, despite life's ups and downs and our normal mood fluctuations. When we seek this type of happiness, it's easier to make a good decision because we're acting to give ourselves something rather than withholding something—an attitude of moving toward rather than moving away, embracing life rather than rejecting it. Moving toward happiness makes us more receptive and open to the joy of living, says this very wise man.

*I can't resist seeking happiness via the living God
who is the author of all happiness. And I can't resist enthusiastically
loving Jesus, who brings us to the Father in such a personal way.*

*I'll look, Lord, not at the things that are wrong in my life, but
at the good you bring into my life, and the good you can extract
from me as we travel together through life. How exciting that is!*

*Phil 4:6-8 talks about peace that passes understanding. It will be mine, I
know, as I ponder uplifting thoughts, pray about everything, and resist
whatever diverts me from picking up my cross and following Jesus.*

What About You?

1. What are you resisting? What are you seeking? How can the seeking eliminate much of the resisting?

2. What are some ways in which we can pick up our crosses and follow Jesus?

3. Hugo and I would like to develop a course on happiness that would inspire others as well as ourselves. What good idea(s) would you like to pursue?

Calm

What a great word to resonate through the coming holidays! At our age we approach Christmas in a much calmer manner. We do very little shopping and gift-giving. We, and all the folks we know, have pretty much everything we want or need. I do feel a little sorry that we haven't set up a tree or made some festive preparations for the big day. Some of my "Christmases gone by" entailed big family gatherings and all sorts of gift-openings (and I love to think back on those), but nowadays it's just the two of us. All of our relatives (even our daughter and family) are far from us, but our dear friend, Julie, has invited us to share their celebration on Christmas Day—no gifts, just the joy of being together. Sounds marvelously relaxing to me!

My card-sending is once again pretty much on the defensive. For those we don't see much I'm sending a photo from our recent visit with family in Florida. And I try to put more than just a signature into the card; a little news and a loving greeting transforms it entirely. I've fallen short on playing any of our many holiday CDs, which contain great music with fantastic orchestras and well-known celebrities. I do hope that next year I can create more enthusiasm and Christmas spirit during these days preceding Christmas. Maybe we'll celebrate with family in Florida—now that will be exciting (seeing the holiday through the eyes of a 2-year old)!

Some of my dearest Christmas memories are of us standing in church holding lit candles as we sing "Silent Night, Holy Night, all is calm, all is bright." That calms me in ways that are difficult to put into words.

Another calming place is our Jacuzzi bathtub, where I can chat with the
Lord, read an inspiring story, recite some Scripture, or sing a song as
I look up at the clouds peeking through the skylight above.

I think of a wonderful hymn: "Be still my soul, for God is on your side."
I also think of Jesus (asleep during the storm) and his words, "Peace
be still!" (Mk 4:39) which calmed the storm—and can calm us, too.

Thanks, three-in-one God, for your calming effect on our lives.
Help us to pass that on to others by our words (and your words), and
by actions drawn from a steady flow of your "living water."

What About You?

1. Even Jesus needed an angel to calm him as he prayed in the garden (Lk 22:39-44). When have *you* needed and received calming?

2. Who do you know (or know of) who exemplifies a calm spirit? How can we follow his/her example?

3. In what ways is God on our side, as the hymn declares? How can we draw closer to God and get more of his "living water" and the calmness/empowerment it brings?

Understand

It's Christmas Eve. We didn't go to our church service because of our sniffling and coughing, but we did find a nice Christmas concert on public television. I'm sure God understands when things like this keep us from attending church. Jesus' life, death and resurrection convince me that God is very understanding, as long as we consistently strive to be in good relation with him. One of my favorite songs from an old Tennesse Ernie Ford record album is called "He'll Understand and Say Well Done" (written by Lucie E. Campbell):

If when we give the best of our service,
telling the world that the Savior is come,
be not dismayed when men don't believe you,
He'll understand and say: Well done!

If when we come to the end of our journeys,
weary of life and the battle is won,
carrying the staff and the cross of redemption
He'll understand and say: Well done!

Five things I often pray for are *wisdom, discernment, humility, understanding and compassion.* I have a long way to go on all of them, but at least I'm going in the right direction when I pray for them. And today's word challenges me to be ready for a year filled with listening, learning, heeding and believing...the understanding will follow, I'm sure. It's so exciting to anticipate what God might reveal to me as the height, depth, and breadth of my understanding expands in the coming year! Maybe I'll better see God's plan, others' needs, and how I can help.

*Thanks, Lord, for your understanding. When I'm ignorant, hard-hearted, and
arrogant I'm not fooling you. As I suffer the consequences I can always
complain and state my case, as the psalmist so often does.*

*I can also plead and bargain with you, as Moses and David did. They didn't
always get what they wanted, but they grew in understanding as they
hashed it all out with you. And Jacob actually wrestled with you!*

*There's so much we don't understand—that's when faith bridges the gap.
We don't have to know it all as long as we know the One who does.
Thanks for being so available as we start a new seek-and-find year!*

What About You?

1. What would you like to seek, find, and better understand in the
    coming year?

2. Who/What is in need of *your* understanding? How can we work
    on being more understanding?

3. Jesus quoted the prophet Isaiah, who said: *These people listen and
    listen but never understand.* In Mk 8:18 Jesus chides his disciples by
    saying *Are your eyes blind and your ears deaf?* What do you think
    Jesus would say to us today?

Step

December 28, 2010

Step up, step out, step back! If I want 2011 to pan out the way I'd like it to, it would behoove me to *step up* and "get my house in order." That means not just my cluttered, disorganized home and office, but my finances, my goals for the new year, and especially my thinking. I can't do everything I want to, so I need to decide what to focus on and how to best accomplish what I set my mind to do. I'm like a ballplayer stepping up to the "plate." I have to assess the present situation and decide if I should try for a well-placed single or double, surprise everyone by bunting, go for a high fly that will enable a teammate to score, stand still and get walked—or go for the home run, even though it increases my chances of striking out.

I should also be prepared to *step out.* Out of my comfort zone if necessary (or by choice)…out of the ordinary—or perhaps out of the crowd, saying (as Isaiah did): *Here am I, Lord. Send me!* I'd love to step out and have a good time, too. Maybe Hugo and I can take a dance class together and get back to one of our great loves: dancing. We even met at a dance, so it's certainly something for us to consider for the coming year.

Step back. That means changing direction, seeing the bigger picture, taking a break so others can prove that we're not indispensable…getting out of the limelight so others can shine. When asked what's the most difficult instrument to play, a great conductor once answered: *Second fiddle. I can get plenty first violinists, but to find someone to play second fiddle with enthusiasm—that's a problem. And without a second fiddle, we have no harmony* [Bits & Pieces].

Right now is a good time to step back and make some harmony.
It's always a good time to think "humble" and contentedly take the
back seat for awhile. Help me, Lord, to do these things more often.

Most of all, I want to be in step with you, so please take my hand.
Help me to do the things in good order—the way you want them done.
I'll bow my knee before I step forward, so I can humbly "hit a homerun."

I'll take just one step at a time, boldly—be it a giant step or baby step.
By so doing I put my faith into action. And that, Lord, is what you call
us to do. It's the greatest thing we can do! Let's do it joyfully!

What About You?

1. How can *you* step out in faith (put your faith into action) this coming
    year? Today? Right this minute? Don't forget to kneel (and pray) first!

2. How should we *watch our steps*, as individuals, families,
    communities, nations?

3. What are some things that need our *Step to it!* (Do quickly and well)
    approach? What is best left up to God?

Value

December 30, 2010

Well, it's been a year of thinking and talking about what I value most—but admittedly, it's what I do and the way I live that counts. Jesus tells a story (Matthew 21:28-30) about a man with two sons. When the father needs help, it's the son we least expect who comes to his aid. The one who spoke nicely and made pretty promises fizzled out on us. It's like me writing such lofty and heartfelt things, then doing what I did today: buying a quart-and-a-half (the new "half gallon") of my favorite full-fat ice cream and eating it all in one sitting!

Thankfully, a new year gives me new hope in myself and my ability to live out my values. Every day (even every moment) is a new beginning, and a new year bursting upon us really gets our attention. I claim to value God and others, a healthy mind and body, being a good example, using time and talents well, and listening to the right voices. What's so frightening is that so often the wrong voices come, not from outside but *inside* me. The idea may come from outside, but it's *my* inner voice that tells me to do it. Then, what I say fades in light of what I do.

This year of self-reflection and inner growth has been cathartic for me—I hope it's been helpful for you, too. I've certainly learned that it's a walk and a process to live our values. We're never satisfied with ourselves, but it's this dissatisfaction that keeps us moving forward, ever trying to do more, do better, and do the Lord/our parents/ourselves proud. Knowing, loving, and applying the Bible helps a lot. The people we meet in the Scriptures are so much like us—flawed and weak, yet welcomed and loved by the One who created us.

*I regret listening to voices that said: "Do you really like that fat boy?"
"Be tough on your students." "Don't get personally involved." "Ignore
beggars who harangue you." "Discipline with a wooden spoon."*

*I say I value my friends, but forget to call back or keep my promises.
I say I value my family, but I annoy my husband and vacillate
between too much or not enough time with daughter and family.*

*Fortunately, though we can feel like we're damned if we do and damned
if we don't, faith trumps it all. We have a God who loves/forgives us, a
Savior who covers our sins, and a Spirit whose voice is the right one!*

What About You?

1. Why are our works so important when faith trumps all? Why should
   we acknowledge and work on our imperfections even though we'll
   always "fall short?"

2. What do you value? How can you better live these values?

3. David sinned terribly, Peter denied he even knew Jesus, and Paul
   admitted he did what he didn't want to do (and vice versa)…yet God
   used them in mighty ways. How did *their* values and God's grace work
   together for good?

Conclude

December 31, 2010

All things this side of heaven must come to an end—and that includes this one-of-a-kind "Come, Grow with Me" year, 2010. Am I different? Am I better or wiser? Only God knows for sure, and only time will tell. But I'm grateful to be able to conclude this Word-a-Day journey by asking God to bless all that's been written herein so it, in turn, will bless all who read it.

It's been a challenge finding the time to keep up with it, and even taking my laptop on vacation so I could write then, too. When I'd sit at the computer and it would just pour forth with little or no tweaking needed, I'd be amazed and elated. When it was like pulling teeth, I'd hang in there and put forth the extra effort needed. Other times, when something special touched my heart, I'd wipe tears from my eyes and feel a great sense of relief, fulfillment, and perhaps even joy at being able to relive emotional moments and express my heartfelt thoughts and feelings.

This is not written to win the grammar or presentation award—it's left pretty much as originally written (warts and all), except for some early editing and late tweaking. What we've ended up with is a year in my life as seen from my day-by-day perspective, based on an inspired verb-a-day. It evolved into a discipline that inspired me (and hopefully you, too) to contemplate many worthwhile things, make some changes in my everyday living, and grow joyfully in God's direction.

I conclude this book with a feeling of accomplishment. I did it! And now I lay it at Christ's feet, an offering of love done for his glory.

*It's a work that fits right into my life's goal/mission/purpose: to grow
closer to God each day, to bring others closer, too, and to do all for
God's glory. As this door closes I'm sure new doors will be opening.*

*It's been an honor to write this book, Lord. Now I'm depending on you to
help me find exciting ways to promote and use it for your glory.
I grew wonderfully closer to you through it—I thank you profusely.*

*Thanks also to you, dear readers. My hope and prayer is that it helps you
to better understand yourself and your relationship with our amazing God.
May you find the joy, love, and hope in Jesus that I have found!*

What About You?

1. What endings and new beginnings are now taking place in *your* life?

2. What goal, mission, and purpose do you have (or would like to have)
    for *your* life? [You're welcome to use mine, if you'd like!]

3. How have you grown with me this year? How can you help others
    grow in God's direction, too?

Other Publications by Ruth Tschudin

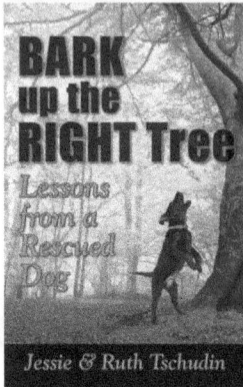

An inspiring, fun-to-read, can't-put-it-down book! Jessie the dog tells the true story of how she is abandoned by her lifelong family, and miraculously teams up with Ruth, a dreamer who pursues an amazing premonition. Lives change and lessons are learned. A 112-page book, available on Amazon.com ($12.95 with 10% supporting animal rescue) and on www.OpenDoorsAGF.org for $5.00 pdf (100% supporting animal rescue).

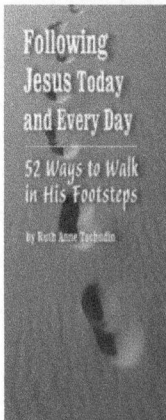

Dedicated to all who seek to live a Christ-like life. The 52 recommendations make it easier to walk in His footsteps—today and every day! 20 pages, 3.5x8.5 inches—fits right into a shirt/pants pocket or a regular size envelope. Great for personal quiet time, Bible Studies, Sunday School classes, prison ministries, and a multitude of other uses. Available on www.OpenDoorsAGF.org; $3.99 for pdf, $4.99 mailed in booklet form. Quantity discounts available.

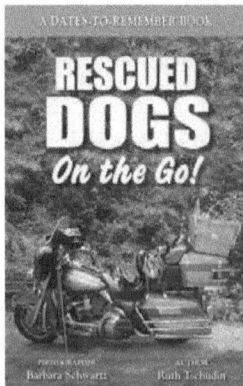

Co-authored with Barbara Schwartz, photographer. Neighborhood rescues pose in a monthly format for this one-of-a-kind dates-to-remember book. All proceeds from this full-color 28-page book will be used by Open Doors, an Amazing Grace Foundation, to support animal rescue. Lots of heart-breaking stories, with happy endings all! Available on www.OpenDoorsAGF.org in pdf form for $5.00; mailed in book form $10.95.

www.ingramcontent.com/pod-product-compliance
Lightning Source LLC
Chambersburg PA
CBHW072002060426
42446CB00042B/1371